ZANZIBAR

The Insider's Guide

ZANZIBAR
The Insider's Guide

Ian Michler

CONTENTS

Author's note

I have wandered often – sometimes wisely and sometimes waywardly. Whichever the case, my immediate family have always understood and accepted my course with love and support. I am truly blessed. To Alison, my mother, and Janet and Anthony, my sister and brother: this work is dedicated to you.

In my wanderings, I have been fortunate to spend much time in Zanzibar, one of Africa's most appealing destinations. This book is hopefully representative of the joys and inspiration these islands give to those that visit their shores. It has been with the assistance and support of others that I have been able to complete this project. My sincere thanks and gratitude go to them for their generous efforts. All of them contribute hugely to making Zanzibar and Pemba the incredible places they are.

In Zanzibar, Christine Henry at ZanTours for enthusiastically embracing the project from the very beginning and for her organisational input; Abdalla Rashid Abdalla and Arun Polanis for their hospitality and

friendship during my stay at the Chavda Hotel; Ali Pillow from Forodhani Car Hire for assisting with my transport requirements; Waldemar Müggenburg and Stefanie Schötz from Mtoni Marine Centre; Abdul Rahim at Memories of Zanzibar; Karin Öljemark, Jane and Alastair Norton-Griffiths and Annette and Mark Sinagra from Matemwe Bungalows; Elly Mlang'a at Shooting Star Lodge; Saleh and Hassan Said from Mercury's; Stephanie Hill from the Dharma Lounge and the Garage Club; Eleanor Griplas from Safari Blue; Maurice Turner and Hannes Wolters from Fundu Lagoon; Pascal Bogaert and Anita Sitta from Real Art; Helen Peeks from Chumbe Island Coral Park; Captain Omar and Nick Humphreys at Tropical Air; Fellician Mabunda and Yvonne Owuor from ZIFF; Mohamed 'Eddy' Issa and Yusuf Ramadhan Khamis for looking after me in and around Stone Town. And to Anna for her beautiful smile.

In South Africa, Sharon and Ian McCallum for their input that keeps my writing intelligible; Russell Juds for his early morning photographic expertise; Rodger Williams at African Encounters and Shayne Richardson at CC Africa. In the production of this book, Dominique le Roux, Lesley Hay-Whitton, Erika Bornman and Alison Day (and the rest of the production team) at Struik Publishers for their creativity and hard work. Lastly to Ian McMillan, one of my partners at Invent Africa, for his complete understanding that I spent so much time out of the office, and Gavin Douglas-Hamilton for his immense support and friendship and for joining me on my final week's swing through Zanzibar.

PAGE 1: A square door frame is a typical Arabic influence in Swahili architecture.
PAGE 2–3: A large cargo-carrying dhow, known as a *jahazi*, sets sail from Stone Town.
PAGE 4: Dive boats lying at anchor off Mnemba Island – the large one is a converted dhow.
OPPOSITE: Ornately carved doors, with brass studs and clasps, are a feature of buildings in Zanzibar.

welcome to
ZANZIBAR

Zanzibar is a place of many alluring images. The name alone conjures mystery. It rings of a distant land and brings an immediate association with the aroma of spices and the majestic sailing ship of these waters: the dhow.

LEFT: The beachfront view from the Tembo House Hotel in Stone Town.

'Karibu' Zanzibar

Zanzibar speaks of the romance of lazy languid days spent sun-soaking on **palm-lined beaches** and taking to warm, tropical, azure waters to dive and snorkel at leisure. Adding to the intrigue is the recollection of the mariners who established Zanzibar as the strategic and commercial centre of the Swahili Coast. It was no doubt chosen as a place to settle because of its proximity to the mainland. Traders and slavers, sultans and kings came from the Middle East and the Orient. They were followed in later centuries by European adventurers, explorers and missionaries. Together, they all forged the legendary Swahili nation, its rich culture and a period of wealth and prosperity.

Present-day Zanzibar is revealed in a **stunning palette of colours**. Its character and charm seep from the fading walls of Stone Town's busy alleyways and historical buildings and are visible in the daily lives of the population. The shades of blues, greens and whites highlight the splendour of the coastline. For the visitor, these images are all on display.

But so, too, is the sobering picture of poverty and under-development, exposed in almost every facet of life in both Zanzibar and Pemba. While the marketing images play well in the world of tourism promotion, they trade heavily on the bygone era of prominence that has long since faded. For the citizens of the archipelago, reality now is mostly a life of struggle under circumstances that are little improved since independence. Over 50% of the population live below the **'basic needs'** poverty line. Stone Town, the nation's historical pride, is in urgent need of regeneration, the main airport remains shabby, roads and the general infrastructure are in a state of neglect and the health services are unable to cope with the rate of HIV infection and other diseases.

There are also political tensions to deal with that, if left unchecked, will hamper development and may just fragment the political union of the islands in the future. These concerns – the **political separation from mainland Tanzania** and the disparate manner in which development funding is allocated – divide the people of Pemba and Zanzibar Island. With the seat of local government in Stone Town, it is a fact that Pemba continues to play second fiddle to

Zanzibar Island. Realistically, the separatist ideals are nothing more than an idealistic pipe dream, as the archipelago is unlikely to survive without the umbrella of support that is provided by the mainland Tanzanian government.

There have been pockets of improvement over the last decade, and plans are apparently afoot for various development projects, including Stone Town's rehabilitation and a new airport (these will be primarily reliant on foreign funds and donor agencies). Their contributions and those of the private sector, which has increased substantially in the tourism sector, should not be solely relied upon. It is an open secret that corruption is a factor hobbling progress and, while the local government has been largely unable to provide for the country's ordinary citizens, many of its politicians have become fabulously wealthy.

These realities, though, in no way detract from visiting Zanzibar. It's a place that is at once **exotic and vibrant**, and thoroughly relaxing. And *karibu* is a word you will hear many times during your visit. It's a warm welcome in Kiswahili, and the Zanzibaris truly mean it.

What's in a name?

What is generally referred to as Zanzibar is, in fact, only the larger island of what is the **Zanzibar Archipelago**. The archipelago comprises two major islands, Zanzibar and Pemba, and a number of smaller islands and islets. Located on the southwestern edge of Zanzibar Island is **Zanzibar Town**, the capital and also the only major town in the archipelago. **Stone Town** is the old historical section of Zanzibar Town, and comprises only a tiny fraction of the overall size of the town.

While it is certain the name Zanzibar came from the **Arab traders** who sailed the coast of East Africa from as early as the 8th century, its exact translation has been given various interpretations. Some say it derives from two Arabic words – *zinj*, meaning black, and *barr*, meaning land or coast – that when strung together, as *Zinj el-Barr*, translates into the 'Land or

OPPOSITE: A room with a view of Stone Town in the Emerson & Green Hotel.

LEFT AND RIGHT: Over 95% of the island's population are adherents of the Islamic faith.
BELOW: Women from the Matemwe village take part in wedding ceremonies organised for guests at Matemwe Bungalows.

Coast of the Blacks' in reference to the first inhabitants of the islands. Others prefer the more poetic symbolism that goes with the phrase *Zayn Za'l Barr*, meaning 'fair is the land or coast'.

Because the archipelago, the island and the town all carry the name Zanzibar, the locals often refer to Zanzibar Island by its Kiswahili name of *Unguja* in order to avoid confusion.

The land and its climate

Zanzibar lies in the Indian Ocean approximately 35 kilometres off the Tanzanian coastline or, for those arriving by air, a mere 20 minutes on a scheduled flight from Dar es Salaam to Stone Town. Both main islands, Zanzibar and Pemba, can be seen on a clear day, as can a number of the 50 smaller islands and islets that make up the archipelago.

Pemba is the older of the two larger islands, having emerged from the sea through warping somewhere between 10 and 15 million years ago. While it is politically and economically bonded, this granite outcrop has never been geographically connected to Zanzibar Island.

Over five million years later, Zanzibar Island, the **largest coral island off the coast of Africa**, and its surrounding islets became separated due to the erosion of the headland linking them to mainland Africa. Both main islands have a characteristic coastline of sandy beaches broken by numerous rocky inlets and shallow bays edged with mangrove swamps. Beyond the shoreline, Zanzibar Island is encircled by coral reefs in most places.

The archipelago lies between 4°50' and 6°30' south latitude, and 39° and 40° east longitude. Neither of the islands is particularly large: Zanzibar Island covers 1 666 km^2 and Pemba a mere 988 km^2. Of the remaining smaller islands, Tumbatu in the northwest is the only other one that has permanent settlements on it. Both Zanzibar and Pemba have similar topography with ridges running across the central and western regions of the islands. Their eastern edges are low-lying from north to south. Before the introduction of cultivated crops, tropical lowland forest dominated the islands with dense mangrove forests along their shorelines. The eastern and southeastern regions of Zanzibar Island have a fair amount of shallow-soiled coral-rag that used to be covered with open coral-rag forest and sparse scrub-type vegetation. Today, the **Jozani Forest** on Zanzibar Island and the **Ngezi Forest** on Pemba are the best examples of what the original tropical forests would have looked like. The whole archipelago is low-lying with a maximum elevation of 120 metres.

Lying a short distance south of the equator, the archipelago has a **tropical or equatorial maritime climate** that is primarily influenced by the Indian Ocean monsoons. Warm and humid conditions prevail generally for the entire year and the annual average rainfall is in excess of 1 600 millimetres (Pemba usually receives more rain than Zanzibar Island).

While rain is recorded throughout the year, April and May are the wettest months with up to 320 millimetres per month. July through to September are the driest months. The island has two rain periods: the 'short rains' that fall during November and into early December, and the 'long rains' that fall from late March through to early June.

The coolest months are from June to August with average low temperatures of between 22°C and 24°C, and the warmest months are from November to February with average high temperatures between 30°C and 32°C.

Locally, the hot season is known as *Kaskazi*, and the cooler midyear season as *Kipupwe*. The heavy rain season from March to May is known as *Masika*, and the shorter rain season in November as *Vuli*.

Travel with respect

Over 95% of Zanzibar's population are followers of the Islamic faith, and most adhere to fairly well-defined expectations of social conduct. It is common courtesy to respect their customs regarding dress codes and alcohol consumption. Do not appear in Stone Town or the villages wearing swimming gear or other revealing clothing. **Topless bathing and consuming alcohol in public places are officially prohibited.** While most people are extremely friendly, do ask permission before taking photographs, especially when it is of women; don't enter mosques without permission or before removing your shoes.

be ENTICED

In addition to Zanzibar's exciting history, the exotic and vibrant nature of these tropical islands are what make it such an enticing destination today. There are untold options — mostly extremely affordable — for travellers that take in the sights of Stone Town and the watery delights of its coastline.

LEFT: Romance is an integral part of the Zanzibari experience. Dinner for two at Mtoni Marine Restaurant in Stone Town.

Exotic options

SEE MAPS ON P98 AND COVER — FRONT AND BACK FLAPS

Stone Town ramble

This is one of Africa's historical wonders, and amongst its walls, minarets and spires lies the incredible legacy of East Africa's fabled era of commercial and cultural pre-eminence. The town, the old section of Zanzibar Town, is an architectural delight with almost 2 000 ancient stone buildings reflecting the fusion of its Arabic, Persian, Indian and European heritage. Take to the network of narrow and bustling alleyways and discover neighbourhoods no guidebook has ever mentioned.

A night at Emerson & Green

No matter what budget constraints you have, stretch them and live like a sultan for a night or two in the pick of Stone Town's hotels. It's the ultimate the island has to offer in Zanzibari style. Bedrooms, bathrooms, balconies, passageways and restaurants have all been restored with exquisite authenticity. Time spent in this hotel is a trip back into the history and lifestyle of a more prosperous past.

Sundowners and dinner at Mercury's

Arrive before sunset, grab a seafront table, and spend the next few hours soaking up the Stone Town vibe. Cocktails are always on order and, after a toast to the setting sun, tuck into a menu that offers a seafood fiesta. With stunning views and an island-style ambience, Mercury's is the choice one-stop restaurant and bar for locals and tourists alike.

Sail the islands off Stone Town on *Sabran Jamiil*

For those using Stone Town as their base, get away from the throng on Zanzibar's most stylish dhow. Board the *Sabran Jamiil* and enjoy a fantastic day of sailing and snorkelling around the offshore islands – with lunch and drinks included – before heading back at sunset.

Chumbe Island Coral Park

This rustic island hideaway is a must, preferably for a night or two. With its spectacular coral garden and near-pristine forest reserve, Chumbe Island Coral Park is the pride of Zanzibar's natural heritage and complements the vast savannah ecosystems of mainland Tanzania. Everything about this magical and private island, developed as a fully sustainable ecotourism conservation project, leaves us feeling inspired about the natural world and how we should be co-operating with it.

Matemwe Bungalows

Situated opposite Mnemba Atoll on the northeast coast guarding a promontory of fossilised coral rock, Matemwe is one of the more secluded beach destinations. It's stylish, yet simple – no designer clutter here – just those honest homely comforts and qualities that make you want to stay and stay.

Mnemba Island Lodge

This stunning, recently renovated lodge exudes a sense of exclusivity and is defined by its privacy and sense of style. It lies on a tiny island just off the northeast coast on the spectacular diving reefs of the Mnemba Atoll. The lodge is tucked away in a forest with pristine beaches sweeping its entire shoreline. Whether for diving the days away, as the ultimate honeymoon paradise or merely to relax, Mnemba will suit the dreams of divers, reclusive romantics and sun worshippers alike.

Shooting Star Lodge

Perched high up on a coral rock outcrop, this rustic lodge is Zanzibar's best kept secret. The spectacular sea views alone are worth the very affordable daily rate. Elly Mlang'a is the most engaging of hosts. Throw in the laid-back and intimate atmosphere and you have a gem of a getaway.

Pemba and Fundu Lagoon

Take a Tropical Air charter flight from Stone Town for the 40-minute flip north to the more tranquil and tropical surroundings of Pemba. The island's prize beach and diving destination is Fundu Lagoon. There's a comfortable remoteness here that exudes a sense of exclusivity – something you are unlikely to experience anywhere else in the archipelago. The dense coastal forest that envelops the extremely comfortable lodge – and the most stunning of sundowner decks – only adds to the experience.

ABOVE: Matemwe Bungalows offers
couples a romantic island wedding option.

Ras Nungwi Beach Hotel

The pick of Zanzibar Island's larger beach lodges and hotels, and your best bet on the northern Nungwi tip. Although the lodge is expansive, its size is most definitely offset by the charm and comforts of the surroundings. Divers have access to the superb coral reefs of the Mnemba Atoll and, for the landlubbers, the beaches just stretch forever and ever.

Fumba day trip

A great day trip option is this one south of Stone Town from the village of Fumba. Safari Blue has a number of dhows that take you into the Menai Bay conservation area and offer an excellent chance of

coast. Breezes is the larger of the two and offers all the style, comfort and facilities you would expect of a premier tropical island resort. The Palms, which comes complete with a full spa, is a more private and elegant option and also boasts the most extravagant and luxurious bedrooms on the island.

Festival of the Dhow Countries

If it's carnival time you are after, then travel at the end of June and into July when this annual festival involving the historical Indian Ocean trading nations is held. The whole of Zanzibar comes alive as the cultures of the region merge to showcase their film, music, dance, art and theatre during a week of festivities. While the

close-up encounters with dolphins. Break for some snorkelling and the most sumptuous of seafood lunches on an island before racing for home under full sail in the late afternoon winds.

Breezes Beach Club and The Palms

These two sister lodges lying alongside each other are definitely the prime destinations on the southeast

focus of the festival is centred in Stone Town, the whole of Zanzibar celebrates and travelling acts move across the island, taking the arts to the people

OPPOSITE: The people of the Zanzibar Archipelago comprise an immensely colourful and cosmopolitan mix.
ABOVE LEFT: Sundowners at Fundu Lagoon on Pemba.
ABOVE RIGHT: The old and the new – dhows and ferries.

OPPOSITE: Women collecting shellfish, octopus and sea slugs at low tide.
ABOVE: Fishermen from this village, near Mbweni on the outskirts of Stone Town,
prepare their *ngalawas* for the next day's fishing trip.

OPPOSITE: A warm and traditional welcome to visitors. The sign reads 'Welcome white man'.
ABOVE: A typical countryside scene on Zanzibar Island.

from SLAVERY to SPICES

Despite its size and the fact that it is dwarfed by the colossal continent alongside it, the Zanzibar Archipelago has played a massively influential role in the protracted history of the East African coastline.

LEFT: The main dhow harbour in Stone Town. Most of Zanzibar's building materials and bulk processed foodstuffs are transported to and from here.

Overview

Area	2 654 square kilometre
Population	1.03 million (2002 census forecast)
Density	378 per square kilometre
Population growth rate	3.1%
Total households	184 949
Capital	Zanzibar Town (Stone Town is its historical part)
Principal villages	Nungwi, Paje, Makanduchi, Kizimkazi, Koani and Chake Chake (Pemba)
Independence	10 December 1963 under Omani rule Republic formed with Tanganyika on 27 April 1964
National Day	12 January celebrates the Revolution against Omani rule in 1964
Official languages	Kiswahili and English
Currency	Tanzanian Shilling
Economic growth rate	4%
GDP annual (2001)	US$ 208 million
GDP per capita (2001)	US$ 207.00

▶▶ The people of Zanzibar are known as Zanzibaris, their culture as **Swahili** and their native language as **Kiswahili**. The word Swahili is derived from the Arabic word *sawahil*, meaning 'of the coast'. The Swahili culture and language reflects the mix of African, Arabic and Asian influences on the Islamic people who live along this stretch of the East African coastline.

▶▶ The people of Zanzibar are **predominantly Muslim** with approximately 96% of the population being followers of the Islamic faith (the majority are Sunni). The balance are mostly Christians, Sikhs and Hindus. A percentage of the rural population mixes traditional beliefs with conventional religion.

▶▶ The island has a high degree of **religious tolerance,** with over 60 mosques, four Hindu temples, three Christian cathedrals, a Zoroastrian Fire temple and a Buddhist temple all within Zanzibar Town.

▶▶ Zanzibar is a **semi-autonomous island state** that falls within the United Republic of Tanzania. It is divided into five administrative districts. Three are on Zanzibar Island: South Unguja, North Unguja and Urban/West; and two on Pemba: North Pemba and South Pemba.

▶▶ The archipelago has its own constitution that deals with **internal administration**. Legislature consists of the House of Representatives with 81 members, including the Attorney General. Fifty of its members are directly elected, 10 nominated by the President, 5 are regional commissioners and 15 are appointed women members. The Revolutionary Council (also known as the Council of Ministers) has 14 members who are appointed by the President of the House. The leader of the present government is Amani Abeid Karume.

▶▶ There are **two major political parties**: the Chama Cha Mapinduzi (CCM), with Zanzibar Island as its stronghold, and the opposition Civic United Front (CUF) that has its base on Pemba. The two parties have been at loggerheads since the 1995 elections over the allocation of development funds, election results and separatist issues.

▶▶ Of the **1.03 million** people living in Zanzibar, approximately **395 000** live on Pemba Island.

▶▶ Thirty six percent of the total population live in the **urbanised western regions** of Zanzibar Island, particularly in and around Zanzibar Town where population densities reach 1 700 per square kilometre, and the population growth rates are the highest, at 4.5%. South Pemba boasts 18% of the population and densities of 531 per square kilometre, and North Pemba, 20% of the population and densities of 324 per square kilometre. The lowest densities are found in the south of Zanzibar Island (111 per square kilometre) as this region is the one least suitable for agriculture.

▶▶ Historically, the economy has been a mono-crop one based on the production and export of **cloves**, which provide over 70% of the island's foreign exchange earnings. Tourism, coconut products and seaweed are the next largest contributors. The major trading partners are the United Arab Emirates, India, Singapore, Denmark and the United Kingdom.

▶▶ The largest contributors to **gross domestic product** are the agricultural sector (39%), comprising mostly clove and coconut plantations, public administration (23%), and trade (18%), which includes hotels and tourism. The fishing sector is the largest subsistence sector and the largest subsistence food crops are cassava, bananas, rice and sweet potatoes. Almost 70% of Zanzibar's work force are involved in agricultural or fishing activities in some way.

▶▶ **Tourism** is the fastest growing sector of the economy, with the number of tourist arrivals growing over 650% between 1980 and 2000 (when 97 165 people visited Zanzibar). Italy heads the list of visitors, followed by the UK, USA and Canada, Scandinavia and Germany.

▶▶ Zanzibar has a rather small **industrial and manufacturing sector** for the local market. Most non-food consumables are imported. The largest local contributors are the production and distribution of electricity, the manufacture of cement and lime, the soft drink and mineral water industries, the grain and rice milling industries and the manufacture of furniture and related wood products. The electricity and wood product industries are the sectors employing the largest number of workers. Most of the manufacturing industries are situated in Zanzibar Town.

▶▶ **Education** is free and, although strongly encouraged, is not compulsory. At the last census in 2001, there were 162 primary and middle schools with 168 219 pupils in attendance, and 118 secondary schools with 36 919 pupils. The pupil:teacher ratio was 35:1. Zanzibar also has six colleges and two universities.

▶▶ The percentage of the population living below the **'basic needs'** poverty line as defined by the Millennium Declaration is 51% (2002).

▶▶ Zanzibar's **legal system**, which follows that of mainland Tanzania, is based on English common law combined with the jurisdictions of tribal and Islamic law. The law is administered through a number of subordinate courts: Regional, District, Primary and Juvenile Courts, operating below the High Court. The Court of Appeal sits in mainland Tanzania. Zanzibar has a number of tribunals covering land, housing and commerce, and also has Islamic Courts, which adjudicate on Muslim family issues and certain other civil matters.

ABOVE: The main ferry port and ship harbour of Stone Town. The international airport and seaport in Stone Town are the only official points of entry to the archipelago.

A history based on trade

Although the people of Zanzibar are predominantly Muslim, there is a distinctly cosmopolitan feel to the other aspects of the culture in the island's society. This is a legacy of its long and rich history based on trade. The Egyptians, Phoenicians, Arabs, Persians, Greeks, Indians, Europeans and Chinese have all left their mark on the island and its people.

While most had only a passing influence, the Omani Arabs, Shirazi Persians and Portuguese all settled and ruled – leaving a lasting heritage. Between them they established Zanzibar as the trade centre of East Africa's coastline for almost three centuries.

They came mainly to obtain ivory, slaves, gold, spices and wood in exchange for cloth, cotton wool, porcelain, glass, beads and money.

▶▶ **1000 BC:** The earliest inhabitants of the Zanzibar Archipelago were Bantu-speaking people. They had sailed from the mainland, possibly well over 3 000 years ago.

▶▶ **AD100–1000:** While history does record visits along the East African coast by the Egyptians, Phoenicians and other nations prior to the birth of Christ, the earliest visitors to settle are Arab traders, possibly as far back as the 1st century. By the 8th century they have begun settling Zanzibar Island and trade is occurring on a regular basis. Shirazi traders from Persia arrive during the 10th century. The Swahili culture begins to take root.

▶▶ **1107:** The Kizimkazi mosque is constructed. It still stands today as the oldest building on the archipelago. By the 12th century, Zanzibar has become established as one of the most powerful and influential centres of trade along the coast. It holds this position until well into the 19th century.

▶▶ **1499:** Under Vasco da Gama the Portuguese stop over in Zanzibar on a return trip from India.

▶▶ **1503–1520:** The Portuguese return and settle in Zanzibar, Pemba and along the East African coastline, which they are to control for almost two centuries.

▶▶ **1591:** The English arrive in Zanzibar and establish stopover points on the island for their trade routes to the Far East.

▶▶ **Mid 1600s:** Omani Arabs begin establishing their dominance along the mainland coastline from Mombassa northwards. The people of Pemba rebel against Portuguese control.

▶▶ **1698:** The Omani Arabs defeat the Portuguese. The Al-Busaid dynasty sets about establishing control of the East African coastline using Zanzibar as a base.

▶▶ **1811:** Zanzibar becomes the centre of the slave trade with the opening of the slave market in Stone Town.

▶▶ **1828–1840:** The Omani Sultan, Seyyid Said, arrives in 1828 and establishes the capital of Oman in Zanzibar by 1840. With the prohibition of the slave trade to the south of Zanzibar in 1822, a major source of revenue disappears. Although ivory and slave trading in the hinterlands remains strong, Said begins planting cloves across Zanzibar and Pemba to improve the economic fortunes of the islands. At the height of his power, the Said dynasty controls the coastline from northern Mozambique to southern Somalia and as far inland as central Africa as he establishes an extensive caravan trade. Over 30 000 slaves are leaving Zanzibar per year – predominantly from the mainland interior – while the clove plantations become the world's largest source of this spice.

▶▶ **1841–1845:** The British begin expanding their interests from 1841. With their influence comes pressure for a total end to the slave trade. In 1845 the slave trade is restricted to movement of slaves between the islands and the mainland.

PREVIOUS SPREAD: Bicycles, scooters and dala dala taxis are the principal forms of transport for the majority of the population.
OPPOSITE: Spices, grains and other dry foods are mostly found in the numerous open-air markets scattered throughout Zanzibar.

▶▶ **1856:** Sultan Said dies aboard one of his ships while returning to Zanzibar from Oman. The Sultanate begins to weaken.

▶▶ **1861–1862:** Zanzibar moves to declare its independence from Oman and becomes separated from the Arabic state in 1862. Omani Sultans continued to rule, but under British protection.

▶▶ **1866:** David Livingstone arrives in Zanzibar before setting out to explore the mainland.

▶▶ **1871:** The explorer Henry Morton Stanley arrives on a mission to search for David Livingstone. Stanley returns to Zanzibar in 1872 on his way back to America, after having met up with Livingstone.

▶▶ **1873:** The British force Sultan Barghash to sign a treaty banning the export of slaves. Livingstone dies on the mainland and his body is shipped to Zanzibar before being repatriated.

▶▶ **1886:** The Germans and British formalise their respective territories in East Africa by signing a treaty.

▶▶ **1890:** Zanzibar becomes a full British Protectorate after having its area of control limited to the islands and a short strip of mainland coastline.

▶▶ **1896:** Sultan Hamed bin Thuwaini dies without a family successor to the throne. Prince Khaled, his cousin, claims the throne against the wishes of the British. In order to unseat him, the British bomb the ceremonial palace (now known as The House of Wonders) in Stone Town. It takes 45 minutes to remove him from power in what is listed as the shortest war in history. Sultan Seyyid Hamoud bin Muhammed ascends to the throne with the approval of the British.

▶▶ **1897:** Slavery is finally abolished. The selling of slaves had already been prohibited in 1890.

▶▶ **1913:** Control of Zanzibar is passed from the British Foreign Office to the Colonial Office and it is incorporated into the British East Africa Protectorate.

▶▶ **1961–1963:** Mainland Tanganyika gains full independence from Britain in December 1961. Zanzibar and Pemba become an independent sultanate and member of the Commonwealth in December 1963. Sultan Sayyid Jamshid ibn Abdullah is the constitutional monarch under the Queen.

▶▶ **1964:** In January, the Sultan is overthrown in a revolution that results in 15 000 to 20 000 deaths (mostly Arabs and Indians). The Sultan escapes by fleeing the country. The bloody uprising is led by the Afro-Shirazi Party under the leadership of Abeid Karume, who sets about establishing The People's Republic of Zanzibar. On 12 April, Karume signs a declaration of unity with Tanganyika. The union becomes the United Republic of Tanzania with Karume as its first Vice-President while also remaining President of Zanzibar. He declares Zanzibar a one-party state and nationalises all land. He also confiscates all the immovable property of the Arab population without any compensation.

▶▶ **1967–1972:** Karume survives assassination attempts in 1967 and 1971. In December 1971 he abolishes the post of President and assumes the title of Chairman of the Revolutionary Council of Zanzibar. Lieutenant Humud assassinates Karume in April 1972. He is replaced by Aboud Jumbe who also becomes Vice-President of the union.

▶▶ **1984:** Amid growing discontent over the union with mainland Tanzania and calls for a separation, Jumbe resignes and is succeeded by Ali Hassan Mwinyi. He introduces a new constitution for Zanzibar that includes directly elected members for the island's House of Representatives.

▶▶ **1985–1990:** Mwinyi becomes President of Tanzania in 1985, and is replaced by Idris Abdul Wakil as President of Zanzibar. In 1988, Wakil suspends the Supreme Revolutionary Council fearing that certain members from the Pemba-based opposition party, the Civic United Front (CUF), are plotting to overthrow him. Wakil stands down ahead of the 1990 elections, which are won by Dr Salmin Amour.

▸▸ **1993:** The Union comes under renewed pressure as Zanzibari government attempts to join the Organization of the Islamic Conference (OIC), an act that infringes the Articles of Union and the Union Constitution which established Tanzania as a secular state. The motion is thought to be a signal of protest against the mainland government over the lack of development and financial support given to Zanzibar. The Zanzibari government eventually withdraws its application.

▸▸ **1995–1998:** Dr Amour wins a vigorously contested 1995 election with 50.2% of the vote. The CUF contests the election results and unsuccessfully calls for a recount. Tensions between the parties grow later in the year when the elected members from Pemba refuse to take their seats in parliament and Amour accuses them of plotting to overthrow his government. In late 1997 and early 1998, Amour arrests 18 CUF members, charging them with treason.

▸▸ **2000–2002:** Aman Abeid Karume, the son of the first president, wins highly controversial elections in 2000. These take place under the protection of military forces from the mainland and amidst widescale opposition boycotts. The CUF again refuses to accept the results and accuses the ruling party of rigging votes. Tensions result in demonstrations and clashes with the police during which 40 opposition supporters are killed. In October 2001, the two parties sign a peace accord and the government drops all outstanding charges against opposition members, including the 18 that were charged with treason in 1998.

▸▸ **2004:** Karume continues to lead Zanzibar with the next elections due to be held in late 2005.

BELOW LEFT AND RIGHT: The ruins of the Kizimkazi Mosque, the oldest building in Zanzibar, which dates back to 1107.

ABOVE: The Mangapwami Cave, located about
20 kilometres north of Zanzibar Town, was used to
hide slaves after the legal trade had been abolished.

Black and white gold

If there was one factor that cemented Zanzibar's position as the centre of commercial and political power in East Africa, it was **the slave trade**. This blight, which still stands today as one of the worst 'crimes' against humanity, reached its peak during the 19th century, when over 50 000 Africans a year were captured for sale to colonial masters. Trading caravans would head into the interior regions of mainland Africa to acquire slaves and ivory in exchange for weapons, food supplies, cloth, porcelain, glass and money. During the reign of the Omani Arabs, the trading caravans established Zanzibar as the major port of export for both slaves and ivory.

While slavery may have occurred earlier than the 7th and 8th centuries, the first actual records of trade in African people appear around this time when Arab traders began opening up the trade routes along the East African coastline. History speaks of *Zanj* (Black) slaves being used as soldiers and agricultural or domestic labourers in what is present-day Iraq. Ivory was prized by rulers as a token of stature and historical records show the trade in ivory extending even further back, as far as 2 500 BC, with the Egyptians and Romans being the major buyers. Ivory found its way into Europe via the Middle East but, after 1499 when the Portuguese began taking control of East African trade, its export increased dramatically via all available sea and land routes.

It was not until the commercial demands of both the Arab and European powers during the 17th and 18th centuries that the trade in slaves became a **significant commercial activity**. The rise of Oman led to a demand for slaves to work the date plantations back in the Middle East. And, when the Oman dynasty moved their seat of power from the Middle East to Zanzibar, they required slaves to work the spice plantations and grain fields under cultivation. The Portuguese, French, Brazilians and Indians all became major traders in East African slaves as they sought to supply their own plantation economies with labour.

On the mainland, Yao and Makua chiefs were co-opted into becoming major slavers by procuring people from neighbouring ethnic groups to sell to the passing caravans. This aspect of the slave trade had a major disrupting effect on the continent's traditional life. Tensions between neighbours increased and settlement patterns changed as communities forged strategies to defend themselves against the slavers.

With Zanzibar as the seat of power for the Omani Arabs, it was natural that Stone Town would become the major holding and selling point for slaves. Setting out from the mainland coastal towns of Bagamoyo and Kilwa, **the caravans** would head inland as far as one of the three great Lakes: Lake Victoria, Lake Tanganyika or Lake Malawi. While slaves were the chief bounty, ivory was the icing. The slaves, bound with chains on the return journey to the coastline, would often be forced to carry tons of 'white gold'. Many slaves would die en route, but, for the survivors, the misery was only really beginning. It is said that the town Bagamoyo takes its name from a Kiswahili saying that means '**to lay down your heart**', in reference to those slaves who would know that their freedom was surely over once they reached this point. It was here that they would be chained aboard the massive dhows, known as *jahazis*, for the channel crossing to the chambers and slave markets of Stone Town.

The market took place in what is now the Anglican Cathedral courtyard and began operating in 1811 under the rule of Sultan Seyyid Said. While the traders waited for the arrival of the slave ships, the slaves would be kept in depressingly stark and confined quarters in underground chambers. Many more would die from starvation, suffocation or disease. Before being auctioned off, they were subjected to a lashing while bound to the nearby whipping post in order to determine their physical strength and levels of pain endurance – the stoical ones going for higher prices. Once sold, they were shipped off to a life of hard labour in foreign lands or were kept behind to work the Sultan's spice and coconut plantations on Zanzibar and Pemba. Some estimates suggest that over **600 000 slaves** were sold during the 19th century.

Although a number of European nations had already banned slavery, the beginning of the end of the slave trade in Zanzibar can be traced back to the Moresby Treaty in 1822, which banned the sale of slaves to Christian powers.

The end of slavery

1822: Although the Omani Arabs sign the Moresby Treaty, the slave trade still continues.

1823: Portugal sets 1830 as the deadline to end slavery.

1829: Mexico abolishes slavery.

1834: Britain enacts laws to have slavery abolished in all its colonies.

1843: India abolishes slavery.

1845: Under pressure from the British, Zanzibar officially abolishes slave trading.

1866: David Livingstone arrives in Zanzibar and spreads his anti-slavery message.

1873: Sultan Barghash signs a treaty banning the export of slaves. Under threat from the British, the slave markets are closed down.

1876: Zanzibar signs a treaty denying slave ships entry to any of its ports.

1877: The first service is held in the Stone Town Anglican Cathedral that had been built on the site of the old slave market.

1884: Fourteen European nations and America meet in Berlin to set political boundaries in Africa. They also agree to suppress slavery and promote the ideals of western civilisation.

1890–1897: All forms of slavery finally end in Zanzibar, although it still continues on the mainland into the early 20th century.

One of the major reasons why UNESCO afforded Stone Town its World Heritage status was its 'great symbolic importance in the suppression of slavery... it was a base from which its opponents such as David Livingstone conducted their anti-slavery campaign'.

The Omani Arabs defeated the Portuguese in 1698, an event that allowed them to set about establishing control of the East African coastline using Zanzibar as a base for 266 years. The rule of the sultans began when the Omani capital was moved to Zanzibar in the 1830s and ended with the revolution in 1964.

SEYYID SAID BIN SULTAN (1804–1856) moved the capital of Oman to Zanzibar and set about establishing what is present-day Stone Town. He encouraged America and European nations to set up trading operations in Zanzibar, which resulted in formal ties being established and the opening of embassies. He was also responsible for introducing cloves to the islands.

SEYYID MAJID BIN SAID BIN SULTAN (1856–1870) After a tussle with his elder brother, and with the support of the British, this youngest son of Seyyid Said took control.

SEYYID BARGHASH BIN SAID (1870–1888) The older brother of Majid marked his rule by having the first telegraph cable to Zanzibar laid and establishing a pipeline to bring fresh water to Stone Town. He was also instrumental in having slavery abolished and closing the slave market.

SEYYID KHALIFA BIN SAID (1888–1890) strongly supported the abolition of slavery during his short rule.

SEYYID ALI BIN SAID (1890–1893) Zanzibar became a full British Protectorate under his rule.

SEYYID HAMID BIN THUWAIN (1893–1896) dies without a natural successor.

SEYYID KHALID BIN BARGHASH (25/8–27/8 1896) He claimed the vacant throne against the wishes of the British. Lasting only two days, he was removed from power after the British bombarded The House of Wonders in Stone Town.

SEYYID HAMOUD BIN MUHAMMED (1896–1902) was the British choice for the throne. Britain sent Hamoud's son to be educated in England.

SEYYID ALI BIN HAMOUD (1902–1911) was still a minor when his father died. After travelling to England for the coronation of King George V, he abdicated the throne to live in Europe.

SEYYID KHALIFA BIN KHAROUB (1911–1960) With the aid of the British, Seyyid Khalifa oversaw the construction of the deep water harbour at Stone Town and the first tar roads on the island.

SEYYID ABDULLA BIN KHALIFA (1960–1963) His reign was cut short by illness, and he died from complications caused by diabetes.

SEYYID JAMSHID BIN ABDULLA (1963–12/1/1964) This last Sultan was ousted in the bloody revolution. He escaped to Dar es Salaam and was given exile in the United Kingdom.

OPPOSITE: The Anglican Cathedral, symbolically built over the site of the last open slave market.
ABOVE: The Maruhubi Palace Ruins just outside Zanzibar Town. The palace was built by Sultan Barghash in 1880 as a day retreat.

Present-day Zanzibar is revealed in a stunning palette of colours: expansive sandy beaches, rich coral reefs and clear blue seas.

The clove tree, *Syzygium aromaticum*, is indigenous to the Moluccas Islands of South East Asia and most likely reached Zanzibar via China and the Middle East before Sultan Said Seyyid first introduced it in 1818 as a crop from Mauritius. He viewed cloves as a lucrative additional source of income to his flourishing empire. Grown in similar warm and moist tropical conditions to their homeland, the spices thrived immediately. It took a mere few decades before Zanzibar became the **world's largest producer of cloves**, aided by the abundance of slave labour for the cultivation and harvesting of the plantations.

Zanzibar Island had the most extensive plantations until 1872 when a series of violent storms destroyed most of the crop, leaving Pemba Island as the heart of the clove industry – a position it has held ever since. Because cloves had been such a success, later sultans introduced other spices that included **ginger, cumin, cinnamon, black pepper and lemon grass**.

The demise of the slave trade in the late 1800s meant that spices became the principal economic activity in Zanzibar and, although the islands have long lost their dominant position as the world's leading exporter of cloves, spices still remain the primary source of foreign exchange for the islands.

This may change over the next decade as, since the mid-1990s, tourism has become the fastest growing sector of the economy. With no mineral wealth and an inconsequential manufacturing sector (and agricultural land at a premium), tourism is now viewed in many quarters as Zanzibar's future. Tourists have always been drawn to its mysterious shores, but it was only once Tanzania and the local government moved to liberalise the economy that substantial investment in tourism infrastructure began to take place. Between 1980 and 2000, tourist arrivals grew in excess of 650% and the number of lodges and hotels more than doubled.

The greatest challenge going forward is to ensure that development takes place in an **ecologically and aesthetically sustainable manner**. The self-same space issue that shackles agriculture will, in all likelihood, impact on tourism as the resources that serve to lure visitors – the expansive sandy beaches, rich coral reefs and clear-blue seas – need to be protected. Numerous monstrous resorts have been erected in the last six years, often right next to one another, and there are more to come.

While these types of **developments** may address certain short-term issues such as job creation and an inflow of tourism dollars, they will soon pose long-term concerns. Environmental degradation and congestion loom as resources are set to become heavily over-utilised, local communities become alienated as their subsistence needs are passed over to suit the demands of developers, and simple aesthetics become eroded.

The authorities would do well to look to the lower impact models of the smaller lodges that are **in keeping with the island's size and cultural nature**. The developments on Chumbe Island, Mnemba Island and the one at Fundu Lagoon would seem to be far better in the longer term as they espouse the principles of ecotourism.

OPPOSITE: Tourism is the fastest growing economic sector, with arrivals having grown by over 650% between 1980 and 2000.
BELOW: Safari Blue runs days trips into the Menai Bay Conservation area.

STONE TOWN

Stone Town is the historical hub of Zanzibar and the cultural pride of the nation. And so it should be, as it is without doubt the most authentic example of the many Swahili trading towns that were built along the East African coastline during the 1700s and 1800s. While its heyday covered these centuries, an incredible history spanning two millennia has left a heritage that warrants its status as an outstanding World Heritage Site.

LEFT: The Stone Town waterfront, which has been earmarked for a major renovation and upgrade.

part of the capital, Zanzibar Town. With almost 250 000 residents (Stone Town making up no more than 7% of this), the greater Zanzibar Town region is the most densely populated area in the whole of the archipelago.

Jutting out on a tiny wedge-like peninsula, *Mji Mkongwe*, as it is known in Kiswahili, was built on land that was once separated from the adjoining mainland by a tidal creek. Its distinctive character emerged because most of the **buildings were constructed using the coral rock and stone** found throughout the island: hence the name Stone Town. During the late 1800s and early 1900s, the building boom forced many of the poorer classes to set up residence on the mainland side of the tidal zone with bridges and causeways linking the two neighbourhoods. Now filled in and reclaimed, Creek Road runs along the old tidal zone past the Darjani Market and defines the boundary between Stone Town and the rest of Zanzibar Town.

When you arrive from the airport, the distinction between these two disparate quarters becomes obvious. The stark apartment blocks, ramshackle homes and roadside stores and eateries of Zanzibar Town give way to the larger multi-storied whitewashed buildings of Stone Town, while the wider tree-lined main thoroughfare squeezes itself into a narrow lane that snakes into the old town.

Unless you have opted for an out-of-town choice, as a visitor you should always be booked into a Stone Town lodge or hotel.

For the visitor, ancient mosques and Arab mansions, Persian baths and palace ruins, Hindu temples and horrific slave chambers still stand as testament to the early mariners and traders who settled these shores. More recent reflections include Christian cathedrals, colonial and mercantile headquarters and even homes of former explorers and famous rock stars.

Amidst this astonishing collection from yesteryear are a number of really **fabulous hotels and fantastic restaurants** serving the finest seafood. Zanzibar's additional attractions – the countless beautiful beaches, exciting dive sites and exotic palm-fringed islands and islets – lie within easy access of these comforts and conveniences.

No matter how short your stay, it is always worth spending a fair proportion of your time here. Typically, most visitors choose to spend their time at a beach resort with Stone Town allocated a single day trip only. Why not consider reversing this trend and **use Stone Town as a base** from which to explore the numerous offshore islands, mainland beaches and the historical sites dotted all around Zanzibar Island?

Stone Town is often incorrectly referred to as the island's major city. It is in fact only the old **historical**

ABOVE: A view of Stone Town as seen from the Rooftop Bar and Restaurant in the Chavda Hotel.
OPPOSITE: Over 85% of Stone Town's historical buildings show some form of structural decay. Philanthropic groups such as The Aga Khan Trust for Culture and The Ford Foundation are giving financial and technical support to rectify this. On the left are the top floors of the Emerson & Green Hotel that have been renovated.

ABOVE: Stone Town is an authentic example of the many Swahili trading towns along the East African coastline.
OPPOSITE: Stone Town comes alive around midday when school ends for the day. Education is free and, although strongly encouraged, is not compulsory.

Prior to the arrival of the Portuguese in 1499, present-day Stone Town existed as a remote village occupied by local fishermen only. With the Arabs having established settlements mostly on the south side of the island, the Portuguese looked to colonise new ground that could be readily fortified and defended. **The tiny peninsula was perfect**: it was fronted by sea on three sides and cut off from behind by the tidal creek. Although the Portuguese ruled for almost 200 years, there are few remaining signs of their occupation – only parts of a small chapel inside the Old Fort, a pair of cannons outside the House of Wonders and some traditions and Portuguese words that have been absorbed into Swahili culture.

The Omani Arabs saw them off in 1698, and soon began laying the foundations for what is Stone Town today. Their first priority was defending their gains, and so up went the **Old Fort**, providing a centre around which the town could develop. Expansion and growth really set in from the early 1800s, once the Omanis had established firm control (they eventually moved their capital here in 1840).

The island's new-found political and regional prominence caused a **wave of immigration** as Arab and Indian traders and merchants arrived. Within a few decades, the village of Stone Town had taken on a distinctly urban character. Locally, the expanding spice and coconut plantations made Zanzibar the leading exporter of these products, increasing the number of passing ships that needed servicing from Stone Town. With this success came increasing political and commercial interest in the region from the outside world, much of which was focused on the slave trade. The first to establish relations were the Americans in 1833 and the English followed them in 1841. Both nations came to install trade headquarters and diplomatic embassies that would monitor the ban on the export of slaves to Christian nations. **Growing wealth** meant that mansions and mosques went up all along the waterfront, followed by plantation homes and palaces in the countryside.

OPPOSITE: The Conservation Plan has begun to reverse the damage and structural decay of many buildings.

Burgeoning population growth and increasing levels of commerce created a need for civic administration and an allocation of resources to recreational interests. Public buildings and amenities, ranging from tax offices and hospitals to public parks and bathhouses, set the town apart from the mainland settlements. When the explorers and missionaries began arriving, they added further recognition to the already glittering status of the town. Livingstone, Burton, Speke, Stanley and others all used Stone Town as a base from which to launch expeditions into the mainland interior.

Around 1890, the slave trade had come to an end and control of Zanzibar had moved into the hands of the British. As a result, the economic fortunes and political prominence of Stone Town began to wane. During the first part of the 1900s the deep-water harbour, tarmac roads, a postal service and telegraph lines were introduced, but it was generally a quieter period in the town's history. **True political independence** for local Zanzibaris came via the bloody revolution of 1964. But, despite all the optimism, Stone Town entered a **period of decay** and neglect as much of the wealth and most of the skilled labour fled the country in fear of retribution for over 300 years of Arab and European domination. The only developments, the monstrous apartment blocks that now dominate the landscape beyond Creek Road, came about because of new political allegiances forged with the old East Bloc communist world.

The past decade has seen a **resurgence in appreciation for the heritage of Stone Town**. It began back in the late 1980s when the government first embraced a more transparent attitude to its rule. This brought brighter economic fortunes and, more recently, has led to a substantial growth in the tourism industry. These factors helped focus the need for regeneration and lured philanthropic groups such as The Aga Khan Trust for Culture and The Ford Foundation to offer their financial and technical support. Stone Town's historical and cultural status received the ultimate acclaim in 2000 when UNESCO named it a **World Heritage Site**. All these bodies are, along with local government, involved in the Conservation Plan and other programmes to reverse the neglect and structural decay that affects over 85% of the historical buildings in Stone Town.

A synthesis of styles

A feature of Swahili culture is the unique architecture – a synthesis of styles borrowed from the many nations that have influenced the archipelago's history. The Omanis have played the central role, so it is hardly surprising that the **Arab designs dominate** but, over the centuries of conquest, various aspects of Persian, Indian and European design were also assimilated. Although most of Stone Town's buildings date from the 19th century, they still stand today as testament to a bygone era of wealth and prominence. And, while present-day life continues amongst this legacy albeit under far less prosperous conditions, that self-same historical fabric remains intact as if time has on one level somehow stood still. This is the very essence of what makes Stone Town so fascinating.

There was not much variety of local materials, so most of the **buildings were constructed from coral rock and stone, using mangrove and various mainland hardwoods as supports**, all plastered together with mud or lime. The simplified quadrangular and multi-storied framework with courtyard and flat roof of the Arab and Persian world characterise the majority of buildings here. Other than the trademark carved doors, the only other prominent street-level feature was a stone bench, or *baraza*, built along the front outer wall on both sides of the door where families and neighbours whiled away the leisure hours in social chatter. Windows, confined to the top floors, were rather small and always shuttered. Indian merchants began arriving later in the century, many of whom started out by buying from Arab merchants and adding their own design characteristics to the existing homes. Those that built from scratch had a preference for placing a shop on the ground floor with living quarters above. As their family and wealth grew, so they would add to the home, with some placing a tiny 'tea room' extension protruding from the very top for those hot summer days. Intricate balconies and verandas on the upper levels that would extend the length of the walls were prominent features. Fascia boards, some with coloured glazed inserts, added to the ornate façade.

The most significant European influence came around the turn of the 19th century after Zanzibar had effectively passed into British hands. John Sinclair arrived as a young colonial officer in 1896 and, by the time he departed 27 years later, had left an indelible mark not only on the landscape of Stone Town, but also Mombassa and Dar es Salaam. His **mix of Moorish and Muslim architecture** can be seen in some of the town's most prominent public buildings, notably in the National Museum and High Court. Sinclair was also responsible for various residencies, a sultanate palace, the Post Office and other homes throughout the town.

Back then, with space at a premium and before motor vehicles were in existence, the town was built inwards rather than in the linear fashion of modern-day town planning. Some historians have suggested that the reason for building at such close quarters was a way of beating out the intense midday heat and keeping homes cool. Today, it makes for harrowing driving and can be more than confusing when doing the Stone Town ramble.

To get a complete sense of the place, spend an evening dining at one of two sweeping vantage points – the restaurants on top of the Chavda Hotel and Emerson & Green. From here, the compact and clustered nature of the town becomes strikingly apparent, and so too does the profusion of corrugated iron roofs that melt together in a **patchwork of browns and greys**. These were add-ons to the original homes to counter the erosive effects that the region's heavy rains were beginning to have on the soft coral rock.

Although the fortunes of Zanzibar and Stone Town waned during the early decades of the 1900s, it was only after the revolution in 1964 that the buildings began falling into obvious disrepair. Because of political persecution, thousands of Arab and Indian land- and homeowners fled the country, and most of those that chose to stay had their properties nationalised. This was a period of turmoil and flux that saw poorer rural families moving into Stone Town and taking over the vacated properties at low subsidised rentals handed out

OPPOSITE: Young Muslim boys wait patiently in front of a Zanzibari door that displays elements of both Indian and Arabic influences.

Take to the network of narrow and bustling alleyways of Stone Town and discover neighbourhoods no guidebook mentions.

by the new government. Both parties lacked the financial resources and the necessary concern for the town's upkeep, and so structural decay set in. As population densities increased, conditions worsened. Sewage systems, water drainage and lighting became inadequate. According to Prof. A. Sheriff and J. Jafferji in their excellent book *Zanzibar, Stone Town – An Architectural Exploration*, over 85% of the buildings, in the year 2000, were at various levels of deterioration and more than 100 houses had collapsed.

The **Stone Town Conservation and Development Authority** is the body that is tasked with leading the restoration process. With the aid of and in partnership with bodies like UNESCO and private groups such as the Aga Khan Trust and the Ford Foundation, a renewal process is under way. **The Zanzibar and Stone Town Heritage Society**, a community-based rehabilitation programme, is addressing the social and economic realities of Stone Town as most residents live in poverty. By giving them a voice and focusing on education and the needs of the community, the society aims to instil awareness and pride in the cultural value of their town. **The Conservation Plan** has identified four important areas for detailed planning and rehabilitation: the sea front, the Central Market, the port and a new commercial area in Malindi, with a complete waterfront revitalisation programme due to be announced in 2005. This integrated approach also aims at restoring profile buildings in the meantime: the Old Dispensary and House of Wonders for example, and the training of artisans and craftsmen in the appropriate techniques that the restoration and development of a World Heritage Site requires. It's an onerous task to make up forty years of neglect, but one that surely deserves to succeed.

My door tells of my status

Of the various features found in Swahili architecture, the large and magnificently carved doors are the most outstanding. At last count there were over 500 of them adorning buildings in Stone Town, making for the **largest collection** along the East African coastline. While the records indicate that the tradition may go back to the first millennium, and certainly prior to the arrival of the Portuguese in 1499, Sheriff and Jafferji

note that the oldest dated door still in existence dates from the year of 1700–1. It was not until the mid-1700s, when the Omani Arabs began accumulating their wealth, that carved doors became the most significant feature of homes in Stone Town. Being the entrance to the family home, it was the obvious place to make a **social statement**, and so began the practice of installing larger and more intricately carved and decorated doors. The door would tell of the homeowner's religion, wealth and influence in Zanzibari society, by way of the carved features. Needless to say, the most wealthy and influential had the largest and most elaborate doors.

Typical frames were made from hardwoods – usually teak or ebony imported from the mainland and India – and had double doors that opened inwards. Completing the structure would be a centrepiece that extended from top to bottom and covered the door join, a carved lintel – often with inscriptions from the Qu'ran, **brass spikes** on the door panels and a clasp and chain for locking the door from the outside. Arabic doors were more intricately styled and had flat and square lintels, while Indian doors were simpler with arched or semicircular lintels. It was the Indian craftsmen, brought in by Sultan Barghash during his reign from 1870–1888, that introduced brass spikes as decoration. Traditionally, these were used back in India during times of conflict as a defence against elephants and their riders from forcing doors open.

While the size of the door spoke about wealth, the extent of carvings displaying **symbolic motifs** on the shutter component and doorframe would indicate **status**. All doors were carved in some way, but the influential carved theirs elaborately and had claim to certain motifs. The more traditional motifs included fish, usually carved along the bottom and representing the importance of the sea as a major source of food, the lotus flower for fertility, date palms, rosette flowers and frankincense carved on the centrepiece denoting wealth. A linked chain around the edges represented security. In later years, motifs with lions, snakes and other animals were symbolic of strength and power.

OPPOSITE: A typical alleyway towards the back end of Stone Town.

A feature of Swahili culture is the unique architecture – a synthesis of styles comprising Indian (ABOVE) and Arabic (LEFT) influences. RIGHT: Carved doors, with centrepiece motifs of rosette flowers and frankincence, denoted wealth. OPPOSITE: The Stone Town Cultural Centre, formerly known as the Old Dispensary, was restored by the Aga Khan Trust.

Places of interest

SEE MAP ON COVER – BACK FLAP

Forodhani Gardens

Hardly a garden in the true sense of the word, this scant stretch of well-worn grass and a few flamboyant trees on the waterfront opposite the Old Fort is a favourite meeting spot for the locals. Many gather here during the day to unwind, but the most carnival-like atmosphere is on Saturdays and Sunday evenings. The place becomes crowded with families, friends and neighbours who pour from the alleyways to pick up on the weekly social whisperings of Stone Town. For those with strong stomachs, there is always a bonanza of local food delights on offer. Cooked over countless open fires, the kebabs, grilled seafood, fried chips and roasted sweet potatoes can be had for a few thousand shillings, and the choice of fresh fruit is always tempting.

The Old Fort

After almost two centuries of Portuguese occupation, the Omani Arabs recaptured Zanzibar Island in 1698. On the site of a demolished chapel (and using the materials from the ruins), the Omanis built the fort between 1698 and 1701 to defend themselves from the Portuguese and other Arab dynasties. More recently, the fort was used as a railway depot, military barracks and prison before becoming a national monument.

The Old Fort is presumed to be the oldest building in Stone Town. It merits a visit, particularly for the views from the corner turrets, and the arts and crafts stalls inside. But do avoid the so-called cultural dance shows put on in the evenings – they are usually not worth attending.

The House of Wonders

Also known as the National Museum or *Beit el-Ajaib*, this large, white colonnaded building alongside the Old Fort was built between 1870 and 1888 as a ceremonial palace for Sultan Barghash. It became known as the House of Wonders by locals because it was allegedly the tallest building in Central and East Africa at one time. It was also supposedly the first building within these regions to receive tap water, electricity and an elevator. There remain two impressive features: a pair of the largest front doors you will ever enter (8 metres high and almost 3 metres wide), and a three-storey spiral staircase that is as wide as the proverbial barn door.

During the colonial period, the British used the building as their headquarters and, after the revolution in 1964, it served as the Ideological College of the ruling party. There are plans for a total renovation and to have the building renamed as the Museum of History and Culture. The second-floor balcony offers the best views of the waterfront and harbour.

The Stone Town Cultural Centre

Formerly known as the Old Dispensary, this recently restored building was erected between 1887 and 1894. It was the brainchild of Tharia Topan, at the time one of Zanzibar's richest and most prominent Indian residents. Having achieved much success as a merchant, he wanted to contribute to the community by building a hospital. His vision was realised when the first foundation stones were laid in Queen Victoria's Jubilee year. After he died, it was sold and became known as the Old Dispensary because of the dispensary and resident doctor housed on the ground floor. With its highly ornate exterior and prominent balconies, it is something of a landmark building along the waterfront. The Aga Khan Trust began its restoration process in 1994, a full 100 years after the building was first completed.

The Anglican Cathedral

The first Anglican cathedral in East Africa was symbolically built over the site of the last open slave market that was closed down in 1873. At the instigation of Bishop Edward Steere, the bishop of Zanzibar, the altar was placed exactly on the spot where slaves were whipped before being offered for sale. Construction began in 1874 and the first service was held on Christmas Day in 1877 – despite an incomplete roof. Legend has it that the crucifix was constructed from wood taken from the tree in Zambia under which David Livingstone's heart is buried. The old slave chambers are situated beneath an adjacent building and there is a slave memorial in the Cathedral's gardens.

St Joseph's Cathedral

With its twin spires visible from most of Stone Town, the Catholic cathedral is one of the most prominent buildings in the town. Designed by M. Berangier (the same architect who designed the Cathedral of Notre Dame de la Garde in Marseilles, France), the cathedral was built by the St Joseph's Mission between 1897 and 1900.

The Palace Museum

Also known as The Sultan's Palace as it was home to the Sultan before the bloody revolution in 1964, this building housed the throne of the Al Busaid Dynasty. Complete with a cemetery with tombs of past sultans, it is now a museum chronicling the history of the Zanzibar sultanate from the early 1800s. It is well worth a visit.

The National Museum

Also called the Peace Memorial Museum, it was built in honour of those who lost their lives in the First World War. This intriguing building, set in its own garden at the back of Stone Town, is like no other on the island. Designed by the Englishman John Sinclair and completed in 1923, it brings together many of the architectural styles of the island in one large domed temple-like structure. As the National Museum, it records the history of the island until independence and has a motley natural history collection in a smaller annexe building opposite the garden. This building is set to become the national library when the House of Wonders becomes the main museum.

OPPOSITE: The House of Wonders, once a sultan's palace, is now a museum. Plans are afoot for its renovation.

Darajani bazaar and market

This is the island's biggest and most bustling market – it runs along Creek Road and marks the back end of Stone Town.

It's abuzz with activity, particularly in the early mornings when hawkers and traders arrive from the rural villages and coastal towns with consignments of fresh fruit, vegetables and fish.

Across the road is the bazaar and main *dala dala* taxi terminus, which is definitely worth a visit as it offers an insight into the lifestyles and struggles faced by the majority of the island's population. Most stall holders and patrons are friendly, but do ask permission before taking photographs and take extra care of your belongings.

ABOVE: Stall holders at the Darajani Market, the largest and busiest on Zanzibar Island.
OPPOSITE: The twin spires of St Joseph's Cathedral are a prominent feature of the Stone Town skyline.

Malindi Bamnara Mosque

This mosque is the oldest in Stone Town, having been built sometime in the 17th Century. Extensions were done in 1831, 1841 and again in 1890. It is one of only four mosques in Stone Town from the pre-revolution period that have a minaret.

If there is time to spare, ask your guide to take you to the Hamamni Baths, the Aga Khan Mosque, the Hindu Temple, and the homes of David Livingstone and Freddie Mercury.

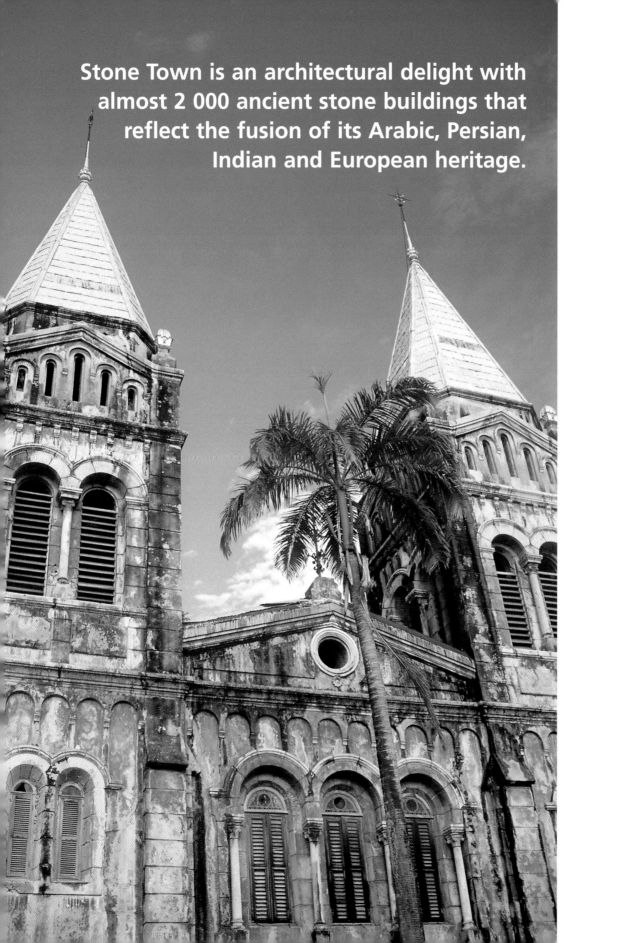

Stone Town is an architectural delight with almost 2 000 ancient stone buildings that reflect the fusion of its Arabic, Persian, Indian and European heritage.

Where to stay

Emerson & Green

This is the pick of hotels, and is situated on Hurumzi Street in the very heart of Stone Town's labyrinth of alleyways. Once an Omani palace, it has been superbly restored, recreating the grandeur and traditions of the past. These uniquely decorated rooms all display the distinctive style of Zanzibar. The hotel has no swimming pool, but three good restaurants. Tel: +255 747 423266,
e-mail: emerson&green@zitec.org

Zanzibar Serena Inn

Top-end hotel on Kelele Square with great seafront views in the quieter section of Stone Town. It has a choice of three restaurants and a swimming pool.
Tel: +255 24 2233587,
e-mail: gmahimbo@serena.co.tz

Tembo House Hotel

Great seafront option with swimming pool. Situated in central Shangani, it is the most convenient for shopping and sightseeing. Tel: +255 24 2233005/2232069, e-mail: tembo@zitec.org

Dhow Palace

Recently restored in typical Zanzibari style, the Dhow Palace is located a few blocks up from Tembo House, its sister hotel, towards the centre of town. No swimming pool. Tel: +255 24 2233012/ 2230304, e-mail: dhowpalace@zenjcom.com

The Africa House Hotel

This landmark seafront building was once the residence of an Arabic royal family before becoming The English Club during the decades prior to the revolution. After the revolution, it was used as a government administrative building. It has been upgraded and is now one of Stone Town's finest hotels. It also has what is probably the most famous sunset rendezvous up in the Sunset Bar overlooking the ocean. If you don't mind hustling for a seat amongst the almost exclusively European backpacker crowd, it's worth a drink or two.
Tel: +255 747 432340,
e-mail: theafricahouse@zanlink.com

Chavda Hotel

A great value-for-money option on Baghani Street just off Kenyatta Road. Has a very spacious rooftop bar and restaurant with the best views and tastiest calamari in town. No swimming pool. Tel: +255 24 2232115, e-mail: chavdahotel@zanzinet.com

Karibu Inn

Comfortable and clean budget option conveniently located just up from Forodhani Gardens and the Old Fort. The choice rooms have air conditioning, but not the dormitory type rooms. Tel: +255 24 2233058, e-mail: karibuinn@zanzinet.com

Coco De Mer Hotel

Another comfortable budget option a few doors up from Karibu Inn. The rooms do not have air conditioning. Tel: +255 24 2230852,
e-mail: cocodemer_znz@yahoo.com

For those that prefer greener surroundings away from the hustle and bustle of town, there are two worthwhile resorts outside of Stone Town. Less costly than the mid-town hotels and with ample space and amenities, both are comfortable options for families.

Mtoni Marine Centre

This rustic option with the best beachfront in Stone Town is the pick of the two. Outside of the low season, has a choice of two restaurants serving superb food.
Tel: +255 24 2250140,
e-mail: zanzibar@coastal.cc

Zanzibar Beach Resort

Situated halfway between the airport and Stone Town, this large resort has the most impressive swimming pool in town and plenty of shaded garden area. Although it is on the seafront, avoid the sea (too polluted) and stick to the pool. Tel: +255 24 2236033/ 2236044, e-mail: bookings@zanzibarbeachresort.net

OPPOSITE CLOCKWISE FROM TOP LEFT: The Tembo House Hotel; outside the Chavda Hotel; the swimming pool at the Tembo House Hotel; a bedroom at Emerson & Green.

Eating out

Eating is central to the Stone Town experience. Most of the restaurants ooze the quintessential laid-back island vibe, and the food is generally fabulous at reasonable prices. The setting sun sinks right across the bay from town, so sundowners are always a prerequisite here. Because most places are within easy walking distance of each other, one can sample from a number of spots before the evening is out.

The choice of food and décor is a cosmopolitan mix of Arabic, African, Indian, Chinese and European, with most places offering great seafood and a variety of spicy dishes.

Mercury's

If you want to stay put for both sundowners and dinner, this is, without a doubt, your best bet. The seafront setting – overlooking the small bay adjacent to the seaport – is superb and the place is always bustling with a mix of locals, ex-pats and tourists. The food is great, and your hosts Saleh and Hassan will fill you in on all the local news over a *shisha* pipe. There is live music on most weekends, which may include traditional *taarab* and *kidumbak* bands. And, yes, it was named after Freddie Mercury, the lead

singer of the rock band Queen, who was actually born in Zanzibar. He started life as Farrokh Bulsara in 1946, born of parents with Indian and Persian origins, and he spent his formative years in Stone Town where his father worked for the British administration. He left at the age of seven, when he went off to boarding school in India before returning in 1962 to complete his last two years of high school education in Stone Town. Freddie and his family moved to London in 1964 in the wake of the revolution. Tel: +255 24 2233076 or +255 742 334412

Monsoon Restaurant

Lounge about on Swahili mats and Persian cushions while sampling from a menu offering great spicy and traditional Swahili and Arabic food. The décor mix of North and East African is stylish and the setting tranquil. It is situated on the seafront adjacent to Forodhani Gardens, and has live music most evenings during the high season. Tel: +255 747 411362/410410

The Tower Top Restaurant

Dine with a crow's eye view of Stone Town from this small and intimate restaurant on the top of Emerson & Green. It's open only for dinner with a set menu of traditional dishes, and diners have the choice of sitting on the floor or taking a table for two. Even though it's pricey, booking is essential in the high season. Tel: +255 747 423266

Chavda Rooftop Bar and Restaurant

This under-rated venue has the best views in town and, together with Chinese, Indian and local dishes, serves great seafood at very reasonable prices. Tel: +255 24 2232115/2231931

Kidude Café Restaurant

Named in honour of Bi Kidude, the legendary Zanzibari *taarab* singer, this café-style option on the ground floor alongside Emerson & Green is one of the best lunchtime options. Tel: +255 747 423266

LEFT: Sundowners at Mercury's.

Terrace Restaurant

Lavish seafood menu from the upper balcony of the Zanzibar Serena Inn. With panoramic sea views, the Terrace is also a worthwhile one-stop sundowner and dinner choice. Tel: +255 24 2233587

Mtoni Marine Restaurant

Arguably the best restaurant in town and a favourite with the ex-patriate community, for good reason: the food is fantastic and the ambience relaxing, which makes the 15-minute ride north of Stone Town well worth it. Waldemar (see below) is your host, and he takes immense pride in the exceptional menu he prepares. Pre-book, and ask for a table to be set up on the sandy beach – the romantics can push that to the waterline. Long and lazy Sunday lunches under the palm trees are also winners. Tel: +255 24 2250117 or 747 430230

Pagoda Chinese Restaurant

Good authentic Chinese food at reasonable prices in Shangani Road just behind The Africa House Hotel. Tel: +255 24 2231758

La Fenice

Italian and seafood on a seafront terrace between the Zanzibar Serena Inn and Africa House Hotel. Tel: +255 747 411868

Passing Show Hotel

In Malindi Street just up from the seaport, this restaurant offers great local fare at unbelievably modest prices. While it wouldn't be classed as a dinner venue, it certainly makes for an interesting lunchtime stop – especially for those wanting to mix with the locals.

Waldemar Müggenberg is the kind of host who adds heaps of atmosphere to a restaurant that already serves excellent food. He manages Mtoni Marine Restaurant, one of Stone Town's finest, and is a master chef and thoroughly engaging host.

In 2000, the Mtoni Marine Centre, consisting of a rather rundown beachfront hotel with a bar-cum-restaurant that served very basic fare, was hardly ticking over. Responding to a friend's introduction, Waldemar flew out from Europe to take a look, saw huge potential in the place, and within four years had worked wonders to the menu and helped turn the fortunes of the hotel around.

He spent almost ten years training and working at hotel management and chefs' schools, mostly in Germany, Holland and Switzerland, and his style could best be described as classical Continental. Since moving to Zanzibar though, Waldemar has built his reputation on 'fusion cooking', which blends his classical training with the delights of the local Oriental and African spices and flavours. He loves the creativity of cooking, particularly dishes with seafood, and also the presentation of the plate, and believes the success of his restaurant has been built on doing this with 'quality and consistency'. Friends and regular patrons speak of his passion, charming humour and

generosity of spirit, and say it is when in the kitchen wrapped in his favourite white apron that he really comes alive.

Waldemar brings the same dedication to his social life that he bestows on his kitchen. He loves eating out with friends in Stone Town, but he also enjoys water sports, and a Grand Prix day in front of the television is never missed.

The word around town is that he plays a wicked bao game, and is rumoured to be possibly the best of the *mzungu* players.

Clubs & shopping

For many, downtime while on holiday is about shopping and hitting the clubs. The options for the late night revellers are limited to a few venues. Shoppers, though, have abundant opportunities to indulge. While most hotels and lodges have in-house outlets with a variety of curios, clothing, books and jewellery on offer, your real money should be kept for the large stores, markets and bazaars of Stone Town where the best buys are available.

RIGHT: It is unthinkable to leave Zanzibar without purchasing at least one khikoi or khanga.

Clubs

Dharma Lounge and Garage Club
Both situated in the same premises opposite the Tembo House Hotel, these two spots offer an all-in-one after-dinner option. With a mix of locals and tourists, you can start in the Dharma Lounge, where the vibe is as serene and cool as the air conditioning, before moving over to the Garage Club disco from around midnight.

Sweet Eazy
This lively venue offers something of everything to everyone: bar, live bands, pool tables, dart boards, a reasonable menu and some intriguing characters who come here just to hang out. Live music is on offer almost every weekend during the high season.

Pirate's Cove
A favourite with tourists, this disco is underneath The Africa House Hotel.

The New Happy Club 2000
Mix with the locals in this dark and dingy bar and dance hall situated around the corner from The Africa House Hotel.

Shopping

The Kenyatta Road and Shangani Street circuit starts at the seafront and heads way up Kenyatta Road – it veers to the right – and into Shangani Road. This circuit route returns via the Zanzibar Serena Inn and Tembo House Hotel. Since this is the busier and more cosmopolitan part of town, the stores are more expensive and are unlikely to allow any bargaining.

Lookmanji Art and Antiques
The first shop on this circuit offers an extensive collection of African artifacts and curios. Collectors should not be put off by the stuffy and overstocked surroundings as time spent browsing may just unearth something of value.

Zanzibar Secrets
Around the corner and a few hundred metres up on the left-hand side is the newest of the large outlets. It has a great selection of materials, carpets and other soft furnishings, as well as jewellery, music and books.

Zanzibar Gallery
The next shop up the road, this large gallery has become something of a landmark over the years with a wide selection of jewellery, clothing, khikois, books, spices and curios.

Memories of Zanzibar
Located opposite the Shangani Post Office, this outlet is also known as 'The Souvenir Emporium'. It is certainly the island's premier outlet and, if you have time for only one stop, make sure it is this one. It offers the most extensive range of clothing, jewellery, books, African music, khikois, materials, wall hangings and general curios. Its tidy, spacious and well-lit layout and extremely helpful staff make for pleasant shopping.

One Way
The next shop up from Memories specialises in khikois and all things made from khikoi material.

Opal Jewelry
A small shop opposite One Way with unique and stylish custom-designed jewellery made with a wide variety of precious and semi-precious stones.

Perfect Gem
Recently opened jewellery store that specialises in tanzanite and other semi-precious stones.

Treasure Trove
In Shangani Street, this store has one of the best collections of custom-made silver and African jewellery.

Gizenga and Hurumzi streets take you right into the hustle and bustle of Stone Town. In most of these stores, bargaining is part of the deal. The further from Kenyatta Road you get, the lower the prices become. Start at the entrance to Gizenga Street (leading off Kenyatta Road just after the Zanzibar Gallery) and there's no telling where you may end up. A note of caution: at the back end of Hurumzi Street you will be entering the rougher part of town, so take extra care over your belongings.

Kibiriti
On the left-hand side, almost immediately after turning off Kenyatta, is one of the more stylish local outlets. Offers clothing, jewellery, furniture, artefacts, batiks and their own top quality line of locally woven khikois.

Double F Antiques and Gift Shop
A wide selection of antiques, jewellery and some Zanzibar chests.

Sasik
A women's craft co-operative that offers a range of pillow covers and wall hangings adorned with traditional Arabic, Swahili and Bedouin designs and patterns. The owner and staff are exceptionally warm and welcoming and will allow you into the room at the back for a peek at the weavers and sewers at work.

Yumi and Show
Towards the back end of Gizenga Street, this store has a great selection of beaded leather sandals and bright raffia bags amongst all sorts of other curios and crafts.

Real Art
Right next door to Yumi, this gallery offers a selection of tinga tinga art and other works by well known Zanzibari artists such as George Lilanga and Hassan Kadudu. Spend some time chatting with owners Pascal and Anita – they have a thorough knowledge of the art scene in Zanzibar.

Asante Arts and Curios
You are now in Hurumzi Street – the haven of tinga tinga painters. Pass through the curios in the front room

to the back of this store where they carry a large selection of this art form. Ask the manager to take you into one of the workshops to see the artists at work.

Noorani Curio Shop
In Sokomuhogo Street, this store has a fascinating collection of old books, most dating to the early 1900s, which originally belonged to the Zanzibar Book Club. Also sells stamps, first-day covers and antique coins.

Al-tamim Curio Shop
Opposite Noorani, with a great selection of custom-made silver, coral, amber and turquoise jewellery.

The Old Fort
There are a number of small stores within the fort offering arts, crafts and curios.

BELOW: Memories of Zanzibar, the island's premier shopping outlet.

ABOVE: The Real Art store in Gizenga Street, Stone Town.
OPPOSITE: Spices, particularly cloves, are the archipelago's major export crop.

Day excursions

Sabran Jamiil

An extremely large dhow, or more correctly a *jahazi*, that has been lovingly restored and fitted out with dozens of Persian cushions, chiffons and mats throughout. Take a sunset cruise or, even better, spend a day of island hopping for the most memorable of sailing trips. Tel: + 255 747 417279,
e-mail: enquire@zanzibarunique.com,
website: www.zanzibarunique.com

Jozani Forest

Zanzibar Island's last remaining tract of indigenous tropical forest lies approximately 35 kilometres from Stone Town on the road to Paje and Kizimkazi. And, unless you are diving or snorkelling in the coral reefs, this protected forest reserve of 607 hectares is probably as much wilderness as you are going to see. The 40-minute ride through the countryside is well worth it. The tall fig, palm, ebony and mahogany trees are home to over 2 000 of the rare and endemic Kirk's red colobus monkeys. While these are usually easily seen, the Sykes monkeys and endangered Ader's duikers are less accommodating. Other wildlife includes hyraxes, squirrels and civets, over 50 species of butterflies and, for the birdwatchers, over 90 species of birds, including the indigenous subspecies, Fischer's Turaco. The forest also boasts 26 endemic shrubs.

Set aside time to take one of a number of nature trails leading into the heart of the forest, where legend has it that the Zanzibar leopard still roams. Habitat destruction is the primary threat to the forest and, in order to counter this, a share of profits from those visiting the forest goes to the surrounding villages. According to reserve staff, the incentive is working, which is another good reason to visit Jozani Forest.

The Spice Tour

Although Zanzibar is no longer the world's foremost producer of cloves, a position it held during the 19th century, spices are still the country's largest foreign income earner. Tours to the central districts of Kidichi and Kizambani take in the sights and smells of the plantations that produce the cloves, vanilla, lemon grass, cardamom, cinnamon and nutmeg, amongst many others. Your guide will also offer you a variety of spices to taste, take you to the drying racks and ensure you get the chance to buy pre-packed bags of your favourite spices from a roadside stall.

Island of Ruins

Zanzibar has a number of ruin sites, which are promoted as day or half-day excursions. Many are within a short distance of Stone Town, although most are not worth visiting unless you are a serious history buff. They are all recognised as national monument sites, but there is no upkeep or restoration programme in place. Those that do merit a visit include the Maruhubi Palace Ruins, the Mbweni Ruins and the Kidichi Baths.

For more information and bookings on these tours, contact ZanTours, e-mail: zantoursinfo@zantours.com or tel: +255 24 2233116

OPPOSITE: The Maruhubi Palace Ruins are situated just outside Zanzibar Town.
BELOW: The Kidichi region is best for spice tours.
FOLLOWING PAGE: Dhows, the romantic sailing ships of Zanzibar's waters.

coast to
COAST

The conventional way to plan a holiday with more than one hotel in mind is to pre-book a choice of accommodation and day trips – complete with all transfers – before arrival. Hassle-free travel then takes place in air-conditioned minibuses and only the roadside along the shortest routes between these destinations is usually seen. Those with a more intrepid spirit can arrive with only the first Stone Town stop booked. Spend a few days absorbing the ways of the island, and then hire a 4x4 or small motorbike and head out. This option is potentially the most rewarding, particularly for those travellers who have time on their side and prefer an element of discovery to their journeys.

LEFT: The extended deck in front of Club Dongwe on the southeast coast.

Getting around

The most reliable place to hire 4x4s, motorbikes and Vespas is in Stone Town (Forodhani Car Hire, allypillow@hotmail.com – their 'offices' are under the trees in front of the Old Fort – or ZanTours, zantoursinfo@zantours.com). It can also be done from some of the coastal villages, but you usually have little or no choice and so could end up with a machine not to your liking.

Once you have the wheels, the journey begins. Zanzibar is such a small island that **all destinations are extremely accessible** and can be reached in a relatively short space of time. Stone Town to Nungwi in the far north, for example, can be done in just over an hour and that's pretty much the furthest place from the capital. You cannot really get lost and, if you do, at worst you will get to see a village or beach that won't be more than a few kilometres from where you thought you were.

Driving in Zanzibar is more about keeping your wits about you than obeying traffic laws, as most drivers on the island seem to have their own set of rules. Adhere to all the basics, take the cautious approach and, most importantly, stop when confronted by a road full of rusty barrels. This will in all likelihood indicate a roadblock where the traffic police may ask to see your **international driver's licence**.

Take a map, by all means, but this will only really help with finding the general direction. In Stone Town and the villages, many streets don't have names; some have more than one name; and those that do have names are usually unmarked. When in doubt about a turn-off in the countryside, stop and ask, as the chances are it's not the one you think it is. The **dirt roads** will be bumpy but, because there is so much to see, it's hardly noticeable. Do not, under any circumstances, drive along the beaches. You may very well end up being arrested and having your vehicle confiscated. Otherwise, travelling around Zanzibar Island is easily done and huge fun.

BELOW: Bananas are for sale at almost every roadside stall you pass.
OPPOSITE: More devout Muslim women wear a long black overdress known as a *buibui*.

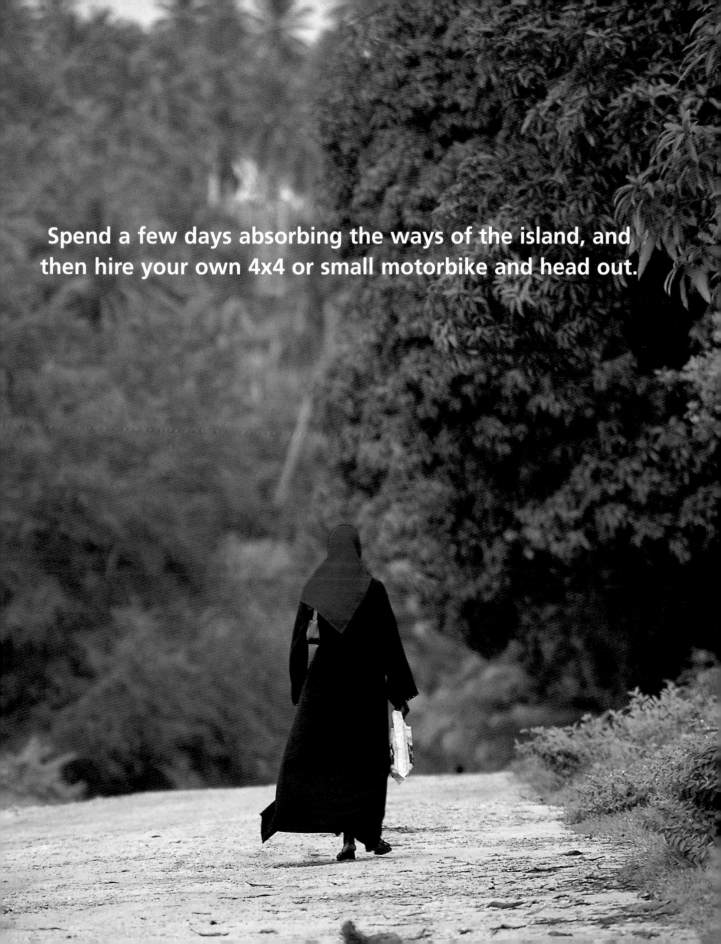

Spend a few days absorbing the ways of the island, and then hire your own 4x4 or small motorbike and head out.

The north

The northernmost tip of Zanzibar is the peninsula of **Ras Nungwi**, an area that many regard as the dhow-building capital of the island. **Ras Nungwi Beach Hotel** on the eastern side of Nungwi is, without doubt, the best option in this region. While this is one of the larger resorts, the relative privacy of the site and the expansive layout amongst terraced gardens are compensatory factors. The seafront rooms have all the modern conveniences, there is a large swimming pool, internet facilities are available and meals are something to savour. With extensive beaches on both sides (and located a boat ride of only thirty minutes from the Mnemba Atoll), the resort is a great choice for those seeking a one-stop destination.

The Ras Nungwi peninsula includes the town of **Nungwi** and its satellite village of **Kendwa**, both of which have gained paradise status amongst backpackers and budget travellers. In particular, the stretch of beach just over a kilometre long on the western edge of Nungwi Village is the real deal for those wanting just to kick back.

The vibe is ever so chilled, and there is an endless choice of budget accommodation, numerous beach bars and restaurants with superb sunset views all within stumbling distance of each other. And it's the perfect hangout for those wanting an effortless stay with internet cafés, tour and diving outlets, curio stalls and mini-supermarkets contained in a single square kilometre of the beachfront. With no coral reefs off the coastline and few mangrove trees in sight, the clincher is some of the cleanest beaches and clearest waters found anywhere in Zanzibar.

Of the many options, **Baobab Beach Bungalows** is the most appealing place to lay your belongings. It offers a choice of clean and comfortable units and also boasts a prime dining and bar terrace overlooking the ocean.

New to the Nungwi scene is a large Italian-owned complex, **La Gemme dell' Est**, which has recently opened. It is situated halfway between Nungwi and Kendwa and, although massive, it is more stylish and luxurious than its east coast counterparts.

BELOW LEFT: The view from Baobab Beach Bungalows.
BELOW RIGHT: Fantastic seafood is readily available at all restaurants.

The east

This region extends from **Matemwe village** down to **Chwaka Bay**, and includes a stretch either side of **Kiwengwa village** that is (rather disapprovingly) referred to by many of the locals as the 'Zanzibar Riviera'. This is not without merit: within a few kilometres of coastline are a number of huge resorts, some right next to each other, that are somewhat out of place on a small island just off the coast of Africa.

Their size is such that some give the sense of being in a large town-house complex somewhere in suburban Rome and their interiors offer little in the way of an authentic Zanzibari experience. That said, places like the **Sea Club Kiwengwa**, **Karibu Venta Club**, **Bravo Club** and **Coral Reef Hotel** may just satisfy your need for holidaying with the crowds.

You will be able to brush up on your Italian though, as it's the language of choice and, for those who love Italian fare, there is no shortage of pizza and pasta on the menu.

The resorts offer a full daily programme of activities for guests, including pool aerobics and beach volleyball as some of the variety of water sports. For evening entertainment, these places have discos, dance halls, poolrooms, movie theatres and all the television you may need. This is also where Italy meets Maasai, as the locals have cottoned on to the commercial benefits of donning traditional warrior gear while hanging out in the hope of a photo opportunity with the tourists.

Not without humour, the hordes of local beach vendors have taken to selling their curios and tinga tinga art (see p136) from stalls that go by such names as Picasso, Gucci and Dolce & Gabbana. Needless to say, these sharp entrepreneurs are pretty much fluent in pidgin Italian as well. Most of the resorts are closed during the low season, usually a week or so after the Easter weekend, and re-open by early July.

The two choice destinations along this coast are **Matemwe Bungalows** and **Shooting Star Lodge**. Small in size, both are without most modern electronic conveniences, have no swimming pool, and have been built in the rustic and unobtrusive manner more befitting the general island-style character of Zanzibar. They also have immense charm and character, and

BELOW: *Tinga tinga art vendors along the east coast.*

ABOVE: This fossilised coral rock formation is at the Matemwe beach.

the water and diving experiences are the order of the day here. For those considering a faraway wedding that comes with the exotic feel of the sea breeze on your face and soft white sand underfoot while the local District Commissioner officiates, Matemwe is one of those perfect choices. It's a service they are proud of offering, and they take care of honeymoon choices as well.

The Shooting Star Lodge is further down the coast and an option that is softer on the pocket. While not as stylised, it has the most expansive beach and sea vistas in the whole of Zanzibar. From its prominent position atop a coral outcrop, it catches the cooling breezes straight off the sea – most welcome during the hotter summer months.

Of the larger resorts, the best on this section of coast is the **Blue Bay Beach Resort**, an incredibly clean and tidy complex within spacious and immaculately kept gardens. It has a great lunchtime dining area right on one of the cleanest beachfronts along this coast. The coastline south of Kiwengwa is not particularly appealing and the **Pongwe Beach Hotel** is the only option on this fairly isolated stretch.

Matemwe Bungalows boasts a complement of the most professional and amiable staff one could hope to meet.

Matemwe has the more private and secluded surroundings of the two, although the nearby fishing villages are within comfortable walking distance. Fantastic food and thorough relaxation amongst all

Elly Mlang'a is the owner and genial host of Shooting Star Lodge, one of the very few locally owned establishments that are successfully competing for the lucrative top-end international market. Although it's been a tough seven years since he first opened, his lodge is already rated amongst the top choices in the smaller, more private and rustic range. Elly now has his sights firmly set on making Shooting Star Zanzibar's most sought-after destination, without ever losing its island-style appeal.

Born and raised in Moshi, beneath the mystery of Mt Kilimanjaro, Elly moved to Zanzibar in the early 1990s. This was after completing his university studies and five years of hard work in the insurance industry in the UK. After a few months in the warm tropical waters, his dream of establishing something of his own came to him. Months of red tape and haggling over a potential site nearly saw him pack it in. But one night (after another fruitless round of meetings with officialdom) and while he was sitting alone on the beach savouring a local brew, the night skies across the ocean lit up with shooting stars. It was an unforgettable night for Elly as he vowed to continue pursuing his dream. This experience gave his lodge its name.

Elly has a great sense of community and is actively involved in numerous spheres within the local Kiwengwa village. 'Tourism will not survive without the support of our neighbours, and it is not right that all this money pours in while they receive little or no benefit,' he says. His commitments are at a financial level and as a board member to various projects including the local soccer team, health and schooling initiatives and crime prevention.

Elly is an engaging and humorous host. If Shooting Star's views and ambience don't grab you, his great personality surely will.

Mnemba Island will suit the dreams of divers, reclusive romantics and sun worshippers alike.

The southeast

Beyond **Chwaka Bay** and extending down as far as **Paje village** is the short strip of coast known as the Southeast. There are a number of hotels and resorts along this section with the **Breezes Beach Club** and **The Palms** being the standout choices. Breezes is large in size, but the stylish design and layout has been sufficiently well thought out to add a sense of privacy. The Palms is right next door and offers a more exclusive and luxurious option. These associated hotels should be on the list of those who seek all the conveniences and plenty of pampering while on holiday.

The nothernmost hotel on this coast is the **Karafuu**, which is also large, with its rooms pleasantly set amongst a plantation of coconut palms. It has, as an added attraction, a lengthy stretch of totally undeveloped beach to one side. Other options include the **Sultan's Palace**, built with Middle Eastern designs in mind, amongst lush gardens, and **Club Dongwe**, anothor hugo rocort aimod at tho Italian markot. Paje village itself is best avoided, as it's exceptionally tacky and the beachfront unappealing. For those with budgets in mind, both **Jambiani**, in the south, and **Nungwi**, in the north, are more attractive alternatives.

OPPOSITE: The village of Kiwengwa on the east coast.
ABOVE: Breezes Beach Club.
BELOW: Coconut fronds are used both as roofing material and to make matting.

The south

It is best to book ahead as these trips are, rightfully, extremely popular. Booking can be made with Safari Blue (adventure@zanlink), your hotel or travel agent.

OPPOSITE: The rural communities of Zanzibar make use of every part of the palm tree. The trunk is used as fire wood and building material, and the leaves as roofing material, oil is extracted from the fruit, the shells are used as cups and rope is made from the fibre.
TOP LEFT: Heading home after a full day of snorkelling with Safari Blue.
BELOW: Rope that was made from the husk of the coconut fruit.

The circuit covering **Jambiani Village** through **Makunduchi** and down to **Kizimkazi** is possibly the most underrated region of Zanzibar Island. Because of this, it has not as yet attracted the attention of the large developers and has the lowest tourism impact levels. This area is best experienced by hiring a small motorbike or 4x4 and taking to the bush track that links these three rural villages. This circuit will allow the most authentic glimpse at how islanders cope with traditional rural country and coastal life.

Kizimkazi lies at the very south of the island and is one of the best spots for viewing dolphins. While the beaches are not of the idyllic palm-fringed variety, they are long and it is possible to take walks without encountering anyone other than local villagers. The oldest building in Zanzibar, the Kizimkazi Mosque that dates back to 1107, is also to be found on its outskirts.

Fumba on the Ras Fumba peninsula in the southwestern region is the starting point for the **Menai Bay** day trips that are run by Safari Blue. The entire bay, in fact, is part of a community-based conservation project run under the auspices of the World Wildlife Fund. The project aims to promote ecotourism while conserving the coral reefs and large populations of Indo-pacific humpback and bottlenose dolphins. The full day dhow excursions include excellent opportunities for dolphin-viewing and snorkelling. A full seafood lunch on one of the smaller islands is also provided.

The offshore islands

Zanzibar Island has a number of small islands within a few kilometres of its shores. Of these, **Chumbe** and **Mnemba** are highlights, while the rest are a bit ordinary. The largest, **Tumbatu Island** off the northwest coast, has no tourist infrastructure at all, and is seldom visited.

Chumbe Island

A mere 12 kilometres from Stone Town lies a tiny island whose standing in the conservation world belies its size: a short 1.3 kilometres in length and only 300 metres wide. **Chumbe Island Coral Park** has been recognised, not only as one of the world's most spectacular coral gardens, but also for the enlightened and fully sustainable manner in which the island's lodge has been developed. Gazetted in 1994 as Tanzania's first protected marine environment, the island's near pristine coral reefs (and the island's forest) are also registered with the UN as a Marine Protected Area. Its natural treasures include over 200 coral species, which is more than 90% of all corals found along the East African coastline, 370 fish species, 120 plant species, one of which (*Uverion den dronekik*) was rediscovered in 1999 after it was thought to be extinct, and over 40 bird species – including the mangrove kingfisher. The endangered coconut crab, the world's largest land living crab species with adults reaching 4 kilograms, is reasonably plentiful here.

The sanctuary was the brainchild of Sibylle Riedmuller, a German environmental education officer who was working in Zanzibar during the early 1990s. Struck by the immense beauty of Chumbe's underwater world, she set about having it declared a sanctuary and developing a small but fully sustainable eco-tourism operation that would conserve the island for generations to come. It took six years of hard work before her vision became a reality. Officially opened in 1998, Chumbe has won numerous international eco-tourism and environmental awards for its model of how conservation, education and tourism can be successfully integrated into one project.

On this 22-hectare island is a still-functioning lighthouse that dates from the late 1890s, with 132 steps to the top, a dilapidated mosque, the main lodge building (that used to be the lighthouse keeper's home) and seven bungalows. The new buildings and renovations have all been completed on sustainable and eco-friendly principles using mostly local building materials and techniques with minimal impact on the surrounding environment. Each building functions as a self-sufficient unit by generating its own water and energy with rainwater catchment and filtration, solar water heating and electricity, and sewage is managed by using composting toilet systems.

A few days here, away from the excesses of the modern world, make for an unforgettable experience.

Mnemba Island

This semi-pristine tropical island paradise lies a short distance off the northeastern coast of Zanzibar Island, an hour's drive from Stone Town and fifteen minutes by boat from Matemwe Village. Zanzibar's most exclusive destination, **Mnemba Island Lodge**, and the atoll's spectacular underwater attractions are what lure people here. The lodge has recently undergone a major renovation with mostly timber and coral-rag being used as the main structural materials. Palm leaf matting, known locally as *makeka*, adds the finer finishing touches. With a rustic yet chic look, and the superbly spacious design, the lodge fits perfectly into its environment.

In order to protect and preserve the atoll's delicate reef environment, Conservation Corporation Africa (CC Africa – the lodge's owners and managers) have, in partnership with the Zanzibar government and the local communities, established the Mnemba Island Marine Conservation Area. The initiative includes a community fund that receives revenues from diving and snorkelling activities and is used to upgrade facilities in the mainland villages and initiate environmental educational programmes that focus on the benefits of eco-tourism.

There is much to preserve here. Besides the countless species of coral and reef fish that occur, the island is an important breeding ground for green turtles. A number of rare species such as hawksbill turtles, whale sharks, guitar sharks and ribbon eels are also found in the atoll's waters. Bottlenose and spinner dolphins can be seen regularly and humpback whales occasionally. On land there are plenty of Ader's duikers and the rare coconut crab to be found.

ABOVE: Fossilised coral outcrops on the
southern fringe of Chumbe Island.

The rest

There are three other small islands off Stone Town. For those who do want to visit them, it is probably best to include all three in one full-day trip of snorkelling or diving. **Chapwami Island**, also known as Grave Island because of several British soldiers buried there, has a small, recently renovated lodge that offers a reasonable alternative to staying in Stone Town. For keen birders, it has one of Zanzibar's only accessible bird colonies consisting mostly of egrets, ibises and storks. **Prison Island**, possibly the most popular of the three with day-trippers, is named after its use long ago as a prison for unruly slaves. Just up from the landing station is a collection of Aldabra giant tortoises that were introduced from the Seychelles a decade ago. The third is **Bawe Island**, a tiny uninhabited outcrop just south of Prison Island.

ABOVE: Mnemba Island Lodge is Zanzibar's most exclusive destination.
BELOW: The only lodge on Chumbe Island.

The coral world

The Zanzibar Archipelago offers divers and snorkellers some of the greatest dive sites found anywhere in African waters. These range from **wall dives, reef dives, coral garden dives and wreck dives**, and are known for their good conditions and variety of corals. The region also has an incredible diversity of other plant and animal species that are attracted to these sites, forming immense underwater communities and food chains. Marine biologists have recorded over 160 families of marine fauna, including close to 3 000 different fish species, in the East African waters.

Conditions can be near-perfect in the prime diving months, which generally extend from **September through to late February**. The continental shelf, although dropping off to depths of almost 200 metres in places, tends to be extremely accessible.

The water of the Indian Ocean is fed by the South Equatorial current that sweeps in from the distant Southeast Asian regions, and is warm and clear with few currents to worry about.

The diving highlights of the Zanzibar Arhipelago would have to be the **Mnemba Atoll, Chumbe Island** and most of **Pemba Island**'s dive sites.

Rainforests of the sea

The coral world is one that goes back over 350 million years. Often referred to as 'the rainforests of the sea', these diverse and spectacularly beautiful ecosystems (although accounting for only a fraction of space in the underwater world) comprise the highest density of living creatures found anywhere in the oceans.

Corals themselves are fascinating creatures that require specific conditions in which to grow. They flourish in the clear shallower waters of the tropics, with average temperatures ranging from 24°C to 30°C, and require plenty of sunlight.

The reefs we seek out for diving pleasure have been intricately formed over thousands and thousands of years by the various colonial hard coral species. As they grow, these massive living structures play host to an immense diversity of other creatures: from microscopic plants to enormous shoals of pelagic fish that are attracted to them for food and shelter. Corals are primitive animals, known individually as polyps,

that over time and under optimum conditions produce a calcareous skeleton for protection. The accumulative effects of millions of polyps living side by side in colonies produce the massive hard limestone structures called reefs.

Of the over 2 500 species of coral found worldwide, over 650 are of the hard coral variety that live in colonies and build reefs. The rest are soft corals that occur in various shapes and sizes resembling fans, branches and flat-topped forms.

The growth of reef-building corals is slow, somewhere between 1 and 10 centimetres a year, and, in order to do so, they acquire over 95% of their food through a symbiotic process with microscopic plants called zooxanthellae that live within the body of the reef corals. The balance of their food comes from capturing various plankton species.

Zanzibar Island dive sites

▸▸ **Mnemba Atoll** While known by this name, Mnemba is not an atoll in the true sense of the word, as the reefs do not completely encircle the island. It is the best known site off Zanzibar Island for it offers the best diving. Although the reefs go by different names depending on the operator used, the dive school at Mnemba Island Lodge distinguishes five distinct sites.

Moon Valley, a length dive reaching depths of 35 metres, is best for viewing green turtles. **Small Wall** has steep drop-offs that attract masses of schooling fish such as snappers, rudderfish and trevallys or kingfish. In between these two dives, lies an extension of Small Wall where plenty of elk-horn and sponge corals occur at depths of up to 25 metres.

The Coral Garden is the most pristine part of the whole reef system with the most impressive variety of corals and a number of angelfish species. **Big Wall** has very steep drop-offs that extend to over 50 metres and is the site for shoals of pelagic fish. Various shark species hawksbill turtles, ribbon eels, frogfish and guitar sharks can usually be seen along the shallower sites of Mnemba.

▸▸ **Chumbe Island** A protected reserve lying just south of Stone Town, Chumbe Island has some of the best coral gardens found anywhere in the archipelago. Reef fish abound, and turtle sightings are common.

▶▶ **Leven Bank** Situated north of Nungwi, this site is for experienced divers. It is best to visit the bank with a reputable operator as the reefs are not easy to pinpoint. It is deep diving and the area usually has strong currents flowing. Highlights include the overall experience of deepwater diving, and plenty of honeycomb and pillar corals on the bank-like reef. The larger pelagic fish species, stingrays, various shark species and groupers are commonly seen here.

▶▶ **Stone Town** Although not as exciting as diving on the northern and eastern edges of the island, the various Stone Town sites are often underrated for medium-level and beginner divers. Most operators visit six main sites that go by various names, and three wreck sites: the **Great Northern**, the **Royal Navy Lighter** and the **Penguin** (which at 40 metres is for experienced deep divers only).

The coral sites – **Bawe Island**, **Nyange Reef**, **Pange Reef**, **Pwakuu**, **Murogo Reef** and **Boribu Reef** – vary in average depth from 10 metres to just below 20 metres. They are all within a short distance of Stone Town and offer great diving with a typical spread of coral and fish species.

▶▶ **Jambiani** There are two sites off this village in the southeast – **Stingray Alley** and the **Jambiani Reef**. As the former's name suggests, the site is well known for the sightings of various ray species, while Jambiani Reef has a large variety of pristine brain and lettuce corals that attract large numbers of the smaller tropical fish species.

Pemba Island dive sites
▶▶ **Misali Island** This is the most accessible site as it lies within a 15-minute boat ride of Fundu Lagoon. It offers fantastic diving at a number of different sites that range from 10 metres to the dramatic drop-off that plunges to depths of over 600 metres. Almost the full diversity of East Africa's coral and fish species is seen here, and the waters between Misali and the mainland offer great dolphin viewing. The management at Fundu

Lagoon are actively involved in trying to establish the region as a protected marine reserve, as its diversity and pristine beauty certainly make it one of the archipelago's must-do sites for keen divers.

▶▶ **Njao Gap, Manta Point and Fundu Reef** There are four reef sites here that lie on the western edge of northern Pemba. The two **Njao Gap** reefs average 15 metres, while the **Southern Wall** at Fundu Reef is a drop-off that goes beyond 40 metres. The highlight is **Manta Point** with its giant manta ray sightings reputed to be some of the most exhilarating worldwide. The sites all have incredible coral reefs and an abundance of both smaller and larger pelagic fish species.

▶▶ **Uvinje Gap** consists of three sites: the **Northern Wall**, the **Southern Wall** and **Kokota Reef**, off the west coast of central Pemba. All three offer spectacular diving and, because of its safety, Kokota is regarded as a night dive site.

▶▶ **Panza Point** includes the coral site, **Emerald Reef**, and a wreck site, the **Southern Wreck**, in the extreme south of the island. The wreck lies close inshore with its top sections showing.

Dive schools
All the major lodges and resorts mentioned in this book will have a dive school, or they make use of the recognised diving operators. For those using Stone Town as a diving base: stick to the larger and reputable operators.

One Ocean Next door to the Sweet Eazy on the seafront, tel: +255 24 2238374 or 0742 750161, email: oneocean@zanlink.com, website: www.zanzibaroneocean.com

Bahari Divers On the Kenyatta Street side of the Forodhani tunnel, tel: 0748 254786, email: baharidivers@hotmail.com, website: www.zanzibar-diving.com

OPPOSITE: *Diving in Zanzibar is reasonably inexpensive and most resorts and dive schools offer beginners' courses.*

The water of the Indian Ocean is warm and clear with few currents to worry about. Near perfect conditions for diving.

Diving with care

The coral ecosystems found within the tropics are under threat. The greatest immediate dangers are pollution and physical destruction. Direct human impacts include oil spills, unsustainable fishing practices such as trawling and the use of dynamite, human sewage, sedimentation runoff and coral collectors, while the indirect impacts are mainly from carbon dioxide build-up in the atmosphere leading to global warming.

Presently, almost 60% of all coral reefs are threatened by human activity in some way and, at the current rate of destruction, scientists believe that 40% of reefs will be destroyed by 2010.

Diving is a growing recreational pastime and, as an increasing number of divers and snorkellers visit the reefs of Zanzibar and Pemba, pressure on the marine environment will grow.

Each individual or group of divers can make a difference to help reduce the stress on these habitats by practising responsible diving procedures. Sadly, it takes between 20 and 100 years for damaged corals to regenerate.

▶▶ Don't purchase any coral from stores or beach vendors (or remove it yourself). It is worth bearing in mind that most countries do not allow the importation of any marine products and, while empty shells and dead coral may look nice on the mantelpiece, purchasing them only encourages the raping of the reefs.

▶▶ We all know not to use coral reefs as a platform to anchor boats. While underwater, take care where you step and be aware of the force created by kicking the fins you wear on your feet.

▶▶ The food humans can provide is not part of the natural diet of fish and such a feeding process will disturb the ecosystem.

▶▶ Resist the natural temptation to 'ride' turtles or whale sharks. This is extremely stressful for these animals.

▶▶ Indo-pacific humpback and bottlenose dolphins are commonly found in Zanzibar's waters, with spinner dolphins occurring around Pemba. Because of the excellent viewing opportunities, the pressure on dolphins is also increasing. Should your operator chase dolphins with his boat, report the company to the relevant authorities. When entering the water with dolphins, do so quietly without jumping or diving from the boat. If you swim after them, they will merely disappear.

OPPOSITE: The Zanzibar Archipelago offers divers some of the best dive sites found anywhere in African waters.
BELOW LEFT: Snorkelling at Matemwe Bungalows.
BELOW RIGHT: Divers from Ras Nungwi Beach Resort head home after a day's diving on the Mnemba Atoll.

PEMBA

Pemba is the northernmost island of the Zanzibar Archipelago, and it's a mere 40 minutes or so in a light charter aircraft or half a day's dhow ride away from Zanzibar Island. The swirling waters of the 60-kilometre-wide Zanzibar Channel separate the two islands. Although less developed and less visited than its southern neighbour, Pemba is as worthwhile a destination. Certainly for the more adventurous traveller in search of remoteness, it is in many ways a superior choice.

LEFT: Low tide off Ras Upembe, Pemba Island's southernmost tip.

The green island

SEE MAP P98

The lush fertility of Pemba is its most striking feature. It also struck the early Arab traders, who named Pemba *Al Khudra*, 'The Green Island' – a phrase still used today by the locals. Unlike Zanzibar Island, a fair portion of Pemba still remains uncultivated with **substantial tracts of mangrove and natural forest** remaining intact. It may not stay that way though, as the palm-lined beaches and evergreen coastal forests that encircle it are rapidly giving way to the subsistence agriculture that dominates the interior. The rolling valleys and slight hills that are so characteristic of the landscape are already becoming blanketed with dense plantations of bananas, cloves, rice paddies and coconut palms. Be it under natural or cultivated vegetation, Pemba has no barren landscapes.

The island is far smaller than its southern neighbour, but it is **geologically older**. Unlike Zanzibar Island, which is comprised mostly of coral rock, Pemba is a granite outcrop that forms part of the continental landmass and dates back to the Miocene age. Much like the main island, Bantu settlers arrived from the mainland centuries before the Shirazi Arabs established the first permanent trading post sometime during the 9th century at Ras Mkumbuu on the island's western side. Next came the Portuguese and, while they managed to take control of Zanzibar Island in the early 1500s, their attempts at subduing the people of Pemba were less successful. What influence they had was broken by the Omani Arabs in the late 1600s, who then ruled under various dynasties until the mid 1800s. In 1890 Pemba and Zanzibar Island became formally incorporated when they both fell under British protection.

FACTFILE

● While the people of Pemba share the same religion and cultural traditions as those of Zanzibar Island, they guard a fierce sense of independence.

● Throughout its history, Pemba's development has always been neglected in favour of that of Zanzibar Island. This disregard has engendered a level of mistrust towards the seat of local government in Zanzibar Town. As a result, Pemba has become the stronghold for the main opposition party, the Civic United Front (CUF). Many Pembans still long for a political breakaway from the mainland.

● Chake Chake is the largest and main town. Other major towns include Wambaa and Mkoani.

● Clove production is the principal economic activity on the island with almost 80% of the Zanzibar Archipelago's total crop coming from Pemba. Bananas, rice and coconuts are the other main crops, with fishing also a major contributor to the island's economy.

● The island has some intriguing cultural aspects. A local form of bullfighting is still practised (the only remnant of the Portuguese occupation). Pemba is known throughout East Africa as having the most authentic practitioners of the African occult, or witchcraft. In keeping with the best traditions of this secretive world, the locals will offer only scant information to outsiders, but it is known that countless people come from the mainland to be cured by, or to learn from, the island's witch doctors.

● There are numerous interesting archeological sites – the oldest dating back to the 14th century. They include the ruins at Ras Mkumbuu in the west, Chwaka in the north, Mtambwe Mkuu in the northwest and Pujini in the southwest. For visits, enquire at Chake Chake or with your lodge management, as unaided access may be problematic.

● The Ngezi Forest, a protected reserve in the far north, is the best example of the natural forest that once covered all of Pemba. It is home to the endemic Pemba flying fox, *Pteropus voeltzkowi*.

LEFT: The town of Mkoani, on the western side of Pemba.
OPPOSITE: Pemba was named *Al Khudra*, The Green Island, by the first Arab traders that arrived in the 9th Century.

There's a comfortable remoteness here that exudes a sense of exclusivity – the sundowner deck adds to this experience.

Fundu Lagoon

Fundu Lagoon is the pick of Pemba lodges, either as an add-on to Zanzibar Island, or as a destination in its own right. It's situated on a low coastal hilltop along the Wambaa Peninsula on the western side of the island. The five beachfront tented units and the nine units set into the hillside have been built into the lush natural forest with absolute minimal impact on the environment.

Boredom is not an option at Fundu. **A full range of water activities** is offered, including diving in uncrowded waters off Misali Island, dolphin viewing, late afternoon dhow rides and water-skiing. Evenings are best enjoyed from the stunning sundowner deck, and meal times are regarded as an activity here. Depending on the tides, superb island cuisine dinners are served either on the beach beneath the palm canopy, or under the stars on the dining deck.

The lodge is run and managed under the principles of ecotourism, and guests have ample opportunity to spend time in any of three villages situated within leisurely walking distance of the lodge. There are another eight villages on the peninsula and all benefit from the Village Fund and **educational training programmes** administered by the senior lodge staff. Fundu Lagoon also offers substantial support to the Misali Island Conservation Fund as a percentage of diving proceeds goes towards this project. Fundu Lagoon is best reached on a Tropical Air Charter (tropic@zanzinet.com) out of Zanzibar Town.

OPPOSITE: The sundowner deck at Fundu Lagoon, possibly the most idyllic spot in the whole of the archipelago.
BELOW: Fishermen from Wambaa, a local village.

Pemba Island

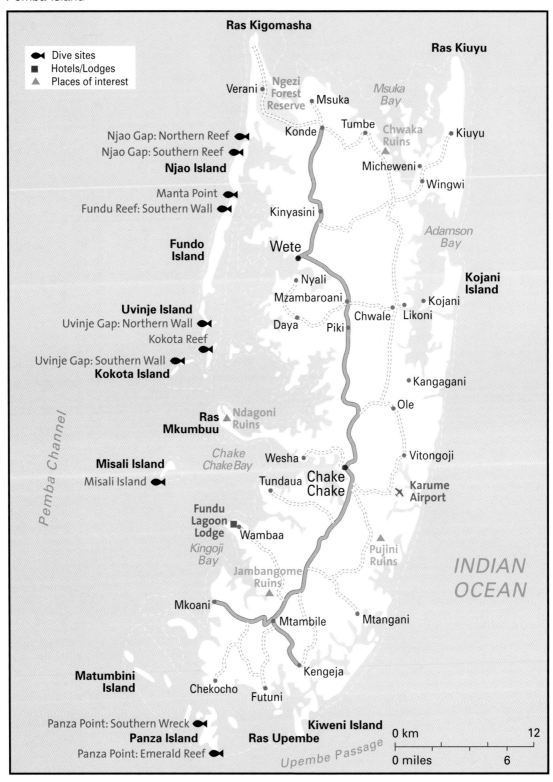

Dive sites
Hotels/Lodges
Places of interest

Ras Kigomasha

Ras Kiuyu

Verani
Ngezi Forest Reserve
Msuka
Msuka Bay
Tumbe
Konde
Chwaka Ruins
Kiuyu

Njao Gap: Northern Reef
Njao Gap: Southern Reef
Njao Island
Micheweni
Wingwi

Manta Point
Fundu Reef: Southern Wall
Kinyasini

Fundo Island
Wete

Nyali
Adamson Bay

Mzambaroani
Kojani Island

Uvinje Island
Uvinje Gap: Northern Wall
Kokota Reef
Uvinje Gap: Southern Wall
Kokota Island
Daya
Piki
Chwale
Likoni
Kojani

Kangagani
Ole

Pemba Channel
Ras Mkumbuu
Ndagoni Ruins

Vitongoji

Misali Island
Misali Island
Chake Chake Bay
Wesha
Tundaua
Chake Chake
Karume Airport

Fundu Lagoon Lodge
Wambaa
Kingoji Bay
Pujini Ruins

INDIAN OCEAN

Jambangome Ruins

Mkoani
Mtambile
Mtangani

Matumbini Island
Kengeja

Chekocho
Futuni

Panza Point: Southern Wreck
Kiweni Island
Ras Upembe
0 km   12

Panza Island
Panza Point: Emerald Reef
Upembe Passage
0 miles   6

Filbert Ngelenge was still scared of water at the age of 25, and certainly not able to swim. Born in Iringa in the southern central regions of Tanzania, he had also never seen the sea. So, when a cousin who was working in the tourism industry in Zanzibar invited him for a visit, he overcame his initial trepidation and took what was a chance in a lifetime for a young man.

Much to his surprise, Filbert felt exhilarated by the expanse of the ocean and decided to take a temporary job on the island before resuming his studies. Six months later, on his way home, he passed through Stone Town and happened to meet one of the directors from Fundu Lagoon Lodge. Having some time to kill, he was persuaded to head north and work at the lodge on Pemba Island. Much to his horror, the job the director had in mind was working in the dive centre. After much persuasion, Filbert agreed to take the position as long as he was not expected to go into the sea.

It was only a few days into his new work when he realised his life was about to change forever. From the outset he felt excited, and after a few weeks of being enthralled at the stories told by returning divers, Filbert's curiosity got the better of him. He took the plunge, and two months later he had learnt to swim sufficiently for his first underwater experience. He became passionately hooked: 'I could not believe what was under the water.' Shortly thereafter he began the beginner's open water diving course and four years later became the first Tanzanian citizen to qualify as a full diving instructor. Still at Fundu Lagoon, he is now one of the senior instructors. Having dived as deep as 40 metres, he counts all the ray species (but especially manta rays) as his favourite sightings.

His hope for the future is that he will be able to introduce diving and the splendours of the underwater world to as many of his fellow citizens as possible.

TOP RIGHT: Filbert Ngelenge, Tanzania's first citizen to qualify as a full diving instructor.
RIGHT: The dive spots around Misali Island are some of the best Pemba has to offer.

the life and
SOUL

Known as Zanzibaris, the people of the archipelago comprise an immensely colourful and cosmopolitan mix. Through the centuries of conquest and settlement, their various ancestors – the fishermen, traders, explorers and travellers who came and colonised these shores – integrated. Together, they forged the heterogeneous society of today that shares the rich and vibrant nature of the Swahili culture.

LEFT: Fishermen lead their *ngalawa* to a mooring point after a day's fishing off Fuji Beach outside Zanzibar Town.

ABOVE: Seaweed farming is a growing industry along the east and southeast coast. Exported mostly to Europe and the Far East, harvesting takes place only two weeks after planting.

OPPOSITE: The central fish market is a focal point in every fishing village.

Coastal life

Life in Swahili societies has always revolved around the sea. While more recent population pressures have necessitated the settling of the island's inland regions, the greater percentage of the population still lives along the coast, subsisting on its wealth of maritime resources. It's a life that is **symbolised by the dhow**: etched across every billowing sail and deep within the wood grains of these majestic sailing vessels of the region. These days the name dhow has become something of a catch phrase for any waterborne vessel under sail. In actual fact, the smaller fishing craft with outriggers are known as *ngalawas*, and the larger sail boats that are used for longer haul transport crossings to Bagamoyo and Dar es Salaam on the mainland coast, and on deep sea fishing trips, as *jahazis*. No matter what their size, they play a central role in the life of Zanzibaris. They can be seen in every seascape along any strip of coastline.

Life on the coast, while idyllic in its setting, is also one of **honest labour**. The land is mostly fertile and the seas are plentiful, and they ensure sufficient food. The tropical conditions, however, bring periods of harsh weather and, like Stone Town, the rural and coastal regions struggle with the burden of under-development. The population must make do with limited water supplies, extremely rudimentary sanitation, poor roads and few health clinics.

Most villages are situated beneath the **extensive canopy of a coconut palm plantation**, and fronting onto a beach. Homes are built from the fossilised coral-rag that is found throughout the island. Limestone, created after subjecting piles of coral rock to the intense heat of log fires, is used as the primary binding agent. Houses were traditionally roofed with banana or coconut thatching. In recent decades, corrugated tin has become the favoured roofing choice for those that can afford it. Outside features often include **simply carved wooden doors** and the familiar coral and cement bench running the length of the more shaded side of the home. Swahili society dictates great respect for women, and their quarters are located in a separate section of the household. Because of a strong sense of community, the homes within a Swahili village almost touch one another and

are separated only by narrow alleyways that lead down towards the sea. There always is a small mosque and the central fish market where the day's catch is landed, and a school of some sort placed on the inland side. The typical village scene is completed with fishing nets and sails laid out for mending, racks of seaweed drying in the wind and a collection of small pens for the few domestic goats and cattle that might be kept.

The men are responsible for the catch of the day, heading out in the *ngalawas* on the falling tide and returning with the incoming tide. **There is ample choice for these supreme mariners**, as, depending on the weather conditions, the haul may include reef fish, shellfish or deep-sea fish. Although species such as turtles and dugongs would have been caught in bygone days, conservation efforts have mostly spared these species from becoming part of the current catch. In some areas along the east coast, men will set out to clear the fish traps or, armed with throw nets, stalk the small bait fish left behind in shallow pools by the receding tide.

The women wade out in the shallows of the low tide to scour the sand flats and exposed reefs for shellfish and octopus. Around Kiwengwa and Bwejuu, women will harvest seaweed for drying, while others will remain in the shade of the palms to make rope or matting from stripped coconut leaves.

The villages of the inland communities have much the same structure, but are often spread out ribbon-like along the edges of the main roads. Each family has an allocated plot of land and grows one or more of the major subsistence crops. In the more fertile regions, bananas, rice, cassava and sweet potatoes grow best, but in the central regions (particularly around Kidichi and Dunga), cloves and a variety of other spices are the primary crops. In the drier southern regions of Makunduchi where the coral rock dominates, the crops of choice are corn, peanuts and sorghum. Small antelope species, such as duiker and dik-dik, are seldom hunted today, as their numbers have been substantially reduced through over-hunting and habitat destruction. Coconuts and other tropical fruits such as mango, papaya and jackfruit grow almost everywhere.

LEFT: Life on the coast, while idyllic in its setting, is also one of honest labour.

Swahili society has always revolved around the sea. Life on the coast might look charming, but it is also hard work.

PREVIOUS PAGE: Coral rock is the principal building material for homes on the islands. The best examples of traditional fishing villages are Jambiani and Matemwe (pictured here). OPPOSITE AND LEFT: Everyday scenes from the fishing village of Matemwe. Any object that won't sink, including old shoes, are used as floats for the nets.

ABOVE: Returning home after a day's fishing.
OPPOSITE LEFT: Catch of the day: tuna.
OPPOSITE TOP RIGHT: Cattle are periodically dipped in the sea to control parasites.
OPPOSITE BOTTOM RIGHT: Collecting shellfish at low tide in Kizimkazi.

PREVIOUS PAGE: Nets are laid out to dry in preparation for the next day's fishing.
ABOVE: Fresh water is in short supply on Zanzibar Island. Typically, villagers walk some distance to designated points in order to collect water.
OPPOSITE: A common sight at low tide on the east coast: fishermen heading home.

A cosmopolitan mix

Although **African, Arabic and Persian influences** are pervasive throughout the population of Zanzibar, a smattering of the European and Oriental exists. The **majority of people are of Bantu extraction** and their ancestral roots extend back mostly to the central and eastern regions of the African mainland.

A sizeable component comprises those of direct Arabic descent, and some who have a mixed African and Persian lineage. Known as **Shirazi**, they trace their heritage back to a Persian prince who fled the Iranian city of Shiraz. They readily inter-married with the local African people, and were the ruling class prior to the arrival of the Portuguese and the Omani Arabs.

Unlike those living on the mainland, the African people of the archipelago tend not to view themselves as tribally divided. If they do draw distinctions, it is primarily based upon their island of birth. On this basis, the majority belongs to the Bantu-speaking **Hadimu** ethnic group, known as Wahadimu or Waunguja, and they are from Unguja or Zanzibar Island. Other ethnic groups include the **Wapemba** from Pemba Island and the **Watumbatu** from Tumbatu Island. Over time, these diverse groups have become amalgamated and, while they may retain certain aspects of their heritage, **life in general is bound by the common Swahili culture.** A small percentage of the population trace their roots back to India and the Orient.

While political and regional tensions have always been present during the synthesis of these diverse peoples, particularly noteworthy is the fact that religious conflict has been absent. Zanzibaris are known to be extremely tolerant of one another's choice of faith.

BELOW: A sizeable component of the population includes people of direct Arabic descent and some, known as Shirazi, who have a mixed African and Persian lineage.

OPPOSITE: Muslims are expected to pray five times a day.

TOP: The headgear worn by devout Muslim women is known as the *hijab*. ABOVE: Shiite Muslims honour the martyrdom of Imam Hussein by lashing themselves to symbolise his suffering.
RIGHT: Midday prayers at the Malindi Mosque in Stone Town.

Zanzibar's lack of religious strife is aided by the fact that approximately **96% of the island's population are followers of the Islamic faith** – a cornerstone of the Swahili culture. The Arab traders who visited the East African coastline from as early as the 1st century brought the religion to Africa. Historians believe it became firmly established somewhere between the 11th and the 12th centuries.

Today, its representation is to be seen and heard throughout the islands: from the **sounds of the early morning or evening calls to prayer** (these are particularly prominent in Stone Town) to the various forms of distinctive clothing that is worn by men and women in everyday life.

Mosques, or *Msikiti* in Kiswahili, are prominent in all villages and throughout Stone Town. They are not only the venues for the five-times-a-day prayer sessions, but also important meeting places for social interaction. The majority of Zanzibaris of African and Arabic descent belong to one of two Islamic sects, the Shafe'I school or the more puritanical Ibadhi school. Those with an Indian heritage belong mostly to various Shia sects.

Muslims believe in the **six articles of faith**: Allah, Allah's word, Muhammed and all the other prophets, the angels, the Day of Judgement and the Holy Books. Muhammed received a number of revelations from Allah, the first of which was one that lasted for 23 years, and was recorded by him in Arabic as the **Qur'an**. Over 10 000 subsequent revelations are recorded in the **Hadith**.

Central to the Muslim way of life is the Islamic calendar, or *Hijri*. Unlike the solar or luni-solar calendars, the Islamic Calendar is based purely on the lunar cycles. The Islamic year also consists of twelve months but, because of the lunar cycles, it is on average 11 days shorter than the Christian calendar and specific months are not related to seasons. All Muslims have an Islamic Calendar in their home, as it is particularly relevant for religious holidays and festivals.

Muslims base the practice of their faith on what is known as the '**Five Pillars of Islam**':

▶▶ **Shahadah** Also know as the Kalimah, the first pillar is the declaration Muslims make to affirm the belief they have in their faith: 'There is no god but Allah; Muhammed is the Messenger of Allah.'

▶▶ **Salah** Prayer is the second pillar of Islam, and must be carried out five times a day. The respected prayer times are as follows: early morning or dawn, noon, mid-afternoon, sunset and at night. The imam, any man within the community who is a scholar of the Qur'an, will lead the prayers. These are held in any clean place, other than the Friday noon prayer, known as Jum'ah, which is usually held in a mosque.

▶▶ **Zakat** The giving of alms is the third pillar of Islam. In the present world, it is more like a tax paid by the wealthy for those less fortunate. In many instances, Islamic law specifies the manner of distribution.

▶▶ **Sawm** The fourth pillar is the practice of fasting. All able-bodied Muslims fast over the period known as Ramadan, the ninth month of the Islamic Calendar. This takes place from dawn to dusk and includes abstaining from food, drink, sexual relations and quarrelling. The fast is completed at the first sighting of the following new moon when a celebration known as 'Id al-Fitr, is held.

▶▶ **Hajj** The last pillar is that all able-bodied Muslims make a pilgrimage to Mecca in Saudi Arabia at least once in their lifetime. Undertaking the Hajj is seen as the ultimate form of worship.

Particular to the Islamic faith is the everyday clothing that is worn by Muslims.

Men wear a long flowing white tunic, known in Kiswahili as a *kanzu*, and a small flat-topped hat, known as a *kofia*.

Women should have their shoulders and legs covered at all times, and the more devout wear a *buibui*, a long black overdress, which may have matching headgear, the *hijab*, that leaves only the eyes exposed.

So to speak

Although both **English and Kiswahili** (also called Swahili) are the official languages of Tanzania, Kiswahili is the most commonly spoken language in Zanzibar. English is spoken in all the popular hotels, lodges and stores, and to some extent by those involved in other aspects of the tourism industry. A minority of the population, mostly those in the older generation, speaks Arabic.

Kiswahili is classified as a Bantu language, and its contemporary vocabulary has been largely influenced by the region's history of conquest and trade as it developed through the centuries primarily as a **common language for commerce**. It now includes many words and phrases assimilated from Arabic, Persian, Portuguese, Hindi and English.

Most linguists distinguish over **10 dialects and some over 15**. *Kiunguja*, the variation spoken in Zanzibar and parts of mainland Tanzania, is accepted as the purest form and forms the basis of Standard Kiswahili. Before the arrival of Christian missionaries, the language was written in Arabic only. The first Kiswahili dictionary using the Roman alphabet appeared in the late 1800s. After Arabic, Kiswahili is the most widely spoken language in Africa with almost five million people in East Africa using it as their first language, and over 60 million as their second language.

It's always beneficial to be able to greet the locals in their own language. For those venturing beyond the established tourist facilities and into the villages, here are some words and phrases that should get you by.

LEFT: Arabic is the language of the Islamic faith.
OPPOSITE: A painting depicting Kiswahili phrases – the language of almost five million people in East Africa .

General greeting – **Jambo** or (more informally) **Mambo**
When greeting elders with respect – **Shikamoo**
How are you? – **Hujambo** or (more informally) **Habari?**
I am doing fine – **Sijambo** or (more informally) **Pao**, which literally means 'cool'
Good or well – **Mzuri**
Fine – **Salama**
Good morning – **Habari za asubuhi**
Goodbye – **Kwaheri**
Good night – **Usiku mwema**
Thank you very much – **Asante sana**
Excuse me – **Samahani**
Please – **Tafadhali**
Can you help me? – **Naomba msaada?**
What is your name? – **Jina lako ni nani?**
My name is Ali – **Jina lango ni Ali**
What is the price? – **Bei gani?**

What time is it? – **Ni saa ngapi?**
Yes – **Ndiyo**
No – **Hapana**
I don't speak Kiswahili – **Sisemi Kiswahili**
Beach – **Baharini**
Mosque – **Msikiti**
Church – **Kanisa**
Market – **Soko**
Police station – **Kituo cha polisi**
Bank – **Benki**
Guesthouse – **Gesti**
Barman, I have a pineapple in my cocktail – **Muhudumu wa bar, nina nanasi kwenye cocktail yangu.**
No, I don't want to buy anything – **Ahsante, sihitaji kununu kitu.**
Why is my scuba tank leaking? – **Ni'kwanini mtungi wa kuzamilia wangu unavuja?**

JAMBO, JAMBO BWANA,
ABARI GANI,
NZURI SANA,
WAGENI WAKARIBISH-WA,
ZANZIBAR YETU
HAKUNA MATATA

Myth & mystery

Belief and its accompanying ceremonies are a vital component of any society. In the Zanzibar Archipelago, these aspects are rooted in traditional African culture, but have been strongly influenced by the Islamic faith.

LEFT: The use of snakes and insects in traditional healing practices and the occult is common throughout Zanzibar and Pemba.

The spirit world

All societies have their darker side and, for the rural people of Zanzibar and Pemba, this aspect of their spiritual world is embodied in the nature of the *Shetani*. Representing all things evil and sinister (those that Christianity would associate with Satan), the *Shetani* is able to **possess its cursed victims** once someone else has cast the spell. To the Zanzibari people who believe in this, possession is very visible. As the *Shetani* takes control of the body and soul, convulsions occur, the eyes roll back into the head and sweating is common. Such a person is left alone – in some cases even ostracised out of fear.

The spiritual world is the domain of the *Mgangas* and *Mchawis*. Both dabble with the wellbeing of individuals and the community but, while the *Mganga* is respected as a **traditional healer** and the purveyor of good, the *Mchawi* is recognized as the witch or wizard that is associated with the *Shetani*.

Inexplicable personal happenings or tragedies are often thought to be the work of the *Mchawis*, who carry out their deeds at night, making use of potions.

No one ever admits to being a *Mchawi*, although many know of each other, so the exact nature of these potions is unknown to the community. They are thought to be mysterious plant and animal-based concoctions. The only recourse for anyone possessed is for their family to approach a *Mganga* for help.

Deemed to be mightier than the *Mchawi*, the traditional healer may have the cure in the form of anti-potions and/or through the performance of symbolic rituals that allow the *Jini*, or good spirits, to return.

As happens throughout the world where missionaries spread the more conventional religions, **Islam, in this case, has become interwoven with the traditional beliefs** of the rural African people. While not all healers do so, many will include the Qur'an as part of the curing process. This takes the form of readings between healer and patient, or may be verses selected and written out on a piece of paper by the healer, to be taken away and read repeatedly by the patient. It is said that the *Shetani* is scared of the words from the Qur'an, and that the *Mchawi*, being a non-believer, does not use the holiest of books.

Rituals to dispossess someone, performed by the *Mganga*, will also include **sacrificial practices**, particularly on the islands of Pemba and Tumbatu. The latter island, situated a short distance off the northwest coast of Zanzibar Island, is shrouded in mystery because of the prevalence of these practices. Goats and chickens are slaughtered and the blood given to victims as a strengthener to fight off the evil spirits possessing them. In some instances, offerings of blood will be made to appease ancestors. Other ceremonies include the use of snakes and insects as healing symbols and a process of smoking out the *Shetani* using a cowhorn filled with smouldering potions.

LEFT: Verses from the Qur'an are often incorporated into the healing process.
OPPOSITE: A *Mganga* and his assistant prepare potions for a ceremony.

Islam has become interwoven with traditional beliefs – it is said that the Shetani is scared of the words of the Qur'an.

ZANZIBAR STYLE

Lengthy white beaches, lofty palm trees and great diving are associated with many tropical islands, but there are certain features about Zanzibar that are unmistakably typical of the island and Swahili culture. Khangas, khikois, the game of bao, the heavily carved doors so prominent in Stone Town, all give one a very definite sense of what can best be described as 'Zanzibar style'.

LEFT: Khanga is the Kiswahili word for the guinea fowl. The material is reputedly named after the bird because the busy patterns resemble the bird's speckled feathers.

Colour and play

Khangas or khikois?

Most conspicuous of all are khangas and khikois, thin rectangular lengths of cotton cloth worn as wraparounds to cover various parts of the body. Decorated with a **profusion of patterns and vivid colours**, both used to be worn purely as functional forms of clothing, but have nowadays become fashion statements in their own right. There is a simple distinction between the two: traditionally, khangas were worn mostly by women and khikois by men. More recently, khangas are worn by locals and khikois by tourists.

Khangas were first utilised as clothing by women along the East Coast of Africa during the middle part of the 19th century and are thought to have originated from the **large handkerchiefs** that were always carried by the Portuguese colonials back then. Swahili women in Mombassa and Zanzibar began buying the scarf-like material, sewing various pieces together to wear over the shoulders and around the waist as large and colourful wraps, usually with matching headgear. They soon became central to the Swahili culture as **traditional wear**, so much so that the khanga is now often referred to as the national dress of Zanzibar. All women own at least one, but usually a variety, with each khanga having social significance in the woman's life. Some are for daily wear, and special ones are worn only at weddings, funerals and other cultural events.

While the bright colours and patterns, ranging from polka dots and paisley to modern designs, are the distinct features, less obvious are the short inscriptions that appear along the edges of most khangas. Usually written in Swahili, these were apparently first introduced by the famous Mombassa trader Kaderdina Hajee Eesak in the early 1900s as a way of boosting sales. The inscriptions originally conveyed **emotional and spiritual sentiments** from the husband or loved one who gave the khanga as a gift. Today, they consist of proverbs and mottos about life in general, and may even commemorate political and cultural events. Some famous inscriptions include: 'I thought you as gold but you are a torment', 'Once you taste pineapple, you will never go for any other fruit', 'My heart is like Sultan, I don't long for any body else's property' or 'Your pleasant scent soothes my heart'.

Khikois, usually slighter longer than khangas and with **distinctly patterned borders**, originated from Arab traders and were worn by fishermen along the East African coast. Today they appear in the markets and stores in a wide range of colours and patterns, and are sold mostly to tourists as beach wear. It is unthinkable to leave Zanzibar without purchasing either a khanga or khikoi.

The game of bao

Played on street corners, along beaches and in village squares throughout Zanzibar, the game of bao is the **most popular board game for the men of the islands**. It is, in fact, so popular that it vies with soccer as the

preferred recreational pastime in many villages. While the advanced strategies of the game are complicated, the basics are simple. So, if you have time to spare, stop by at a bao game and take in a few hours of instruction. You will be welcome, and it's a fun way of getting an insight into the leisurely pace of village life. Bao sets can be bought in the markets of Stone Town, but be sure the board isn't too heavy, and take home extra seeds as some are likely to get lost.

Bao is thought to have been derived from a game brought to the East African coast by Persian traders; it is one of the mancala board games that all originate in either Africa or Asia. Unlike chess or checkers (where carved pieces are moved on a flat surface), these games have seed or bean playing pieces that are dropped into holes carved into the board. Bao is usually played on a heavy board, traditionally carved out of woods such as mahogany or ebony, that has

32 holes (*mashimo*) arranged in four rows of eight, with a front row and a back row for each player. The game plan itself is an **immensely complex and strategic one**. It involves placing the 64 seeds (*kete*) into the holes in an ongoing series of tactical moves.

The aim is either to clear your opponent's front row of seeds by capturing them, or to make it impossible for him to move. Positions can change rapidly, as players alternately gain the upper hand move by move and, although play is fast-moving at times, long periods may pass before a result is obtained.

OPPOSITE LEFT: Khikois are essential beach wear in Zanzibar.
OPPOSITE RIGHT: Bao is a board game played throughout the archipelago. There are numerous clubs that participate in regional tournaments.
ABOVE: Rich colours, so characteristic of khanga material, on display at a wedding ceremony.

Henna painting

Ornate, artistic and fashionable, henna painting is all the rage in Zanzibar. Walk through any of the popular alleyways in Stone Town and you will pass a number of henna salons. It's offered at most lodges and hotels and every beach has a number of painters willing to decorate your hands and feet.

Henna painting has been described by historians as **the oldest art form known to mankind**. This style of body adornment is steeped in the belief systems and spirituality of societies from the Middle East, India and the Far East. With the spread of Islam along the East African coast, henna painting was soon incorporated into the customs of the newly-converted African people.

Henna is extracted from the plant *Lawsonia inermis* by drying and grinding the leaves, which are picked preferably soon after the first monsoon rains. The powder is then mixed with lemon juice and water into a paste to produce the dyes ranging from pale browns to dark russet reds.

While there are many ways to mix and apply henna, the most common method is to add a little sugar, honey or olive oil to add stickiness, before squeezing the paste onto dry skin from the narrow spout of a small cone-shaped appliance. It is lawsone, the hennotannic acid molecule, that leaves **stains on the skin that may last for up to two weeks** before it fades with washing.

Although henna painting remains linked to the **spiritual rituals** that take place around birth, marriage and death, women from poorer backgrounds have also used it as an inexpensive way of adornment, and others as a symbol of luck and fortunate tidings.

Traditionally, only Swahili brides and married women were painted, but today it has also become a fashion statement amongst the youth. It is done for fun by visitors to Zanzibar and many more designs have been added to the more typical floral ones.

THIS PAGE AND OPPOSITE: The spread of Islam brought henna painting to the East African coastline. Traditionally linked to spiritual rituals, it has now become a fashion statement amongst the youth.

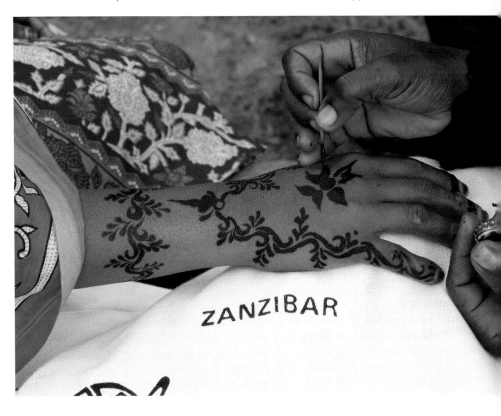

Zanzibari furniture

Walk into any hotel, restaurant, store or home, and you'll notice the distinctive furnishings that add so much charm and character to the interior of the island's buildings. Some of the top hotels, notably Emerson & Green and the Tembo House Hotel, offer classic examples, but most island homes will also carry at least a sampling of the Zanzibar style.

There are a number of defining pieces, all brought to the islands over the centuries by Persian and Arab traders. Pride of place in any bedroom goes to the sturdy **four-poster canopy bed**, covered with volumes of mosquito netting and often decorated with detailed ceramic inlays worked into the headboard. **Zanzibar chests**, solid box-like crates made from the hardier woods and ornately studded with brass work, come in all sizes to store household goods, clothing and finer valuables. Heavier chests remain in the bedroom and kitchen, while the smallest may be found thoughtfully placed on a mantelpiece or at the bedside. Bedrooms and living rooms will inevitably have a collection of four-legged **Omani coffee tables** (mostly with colourful ceramic inlaid tops) hugging the corners. Add an assortment of cabinets, couches and wooden hall stands to the furnishings, which may be complemented with a collection of antique silver and brass ornaments, Oriental porcelain and glassware.

For those smitten by Zanzibari furniture, there are a number of carpenters and craftsmen working from family outlets in the back streets of Stone Town who will make chests, beds and tables on order. Reflect on your impulse, though, as getting the finished product home can be a major challenge.

BELOW: Emerson & Green Hotel offers the most authentic example of Zanzibari style.
OPPOSITE: The entrance hallway to Monsoon Restaurant in Stone Town.

VAN NELLE'S
"TUMBAKU ASLI"
"RISING HOPE "KALI SANA"

MANUFACTURERS
DE ERVEN DE WED. J. VAN NELLE
ROTTERDAM
EAST AFRICAN OFFICE:
VAN NELLE'S OVERSEA TRADING C̊ MOMBASA

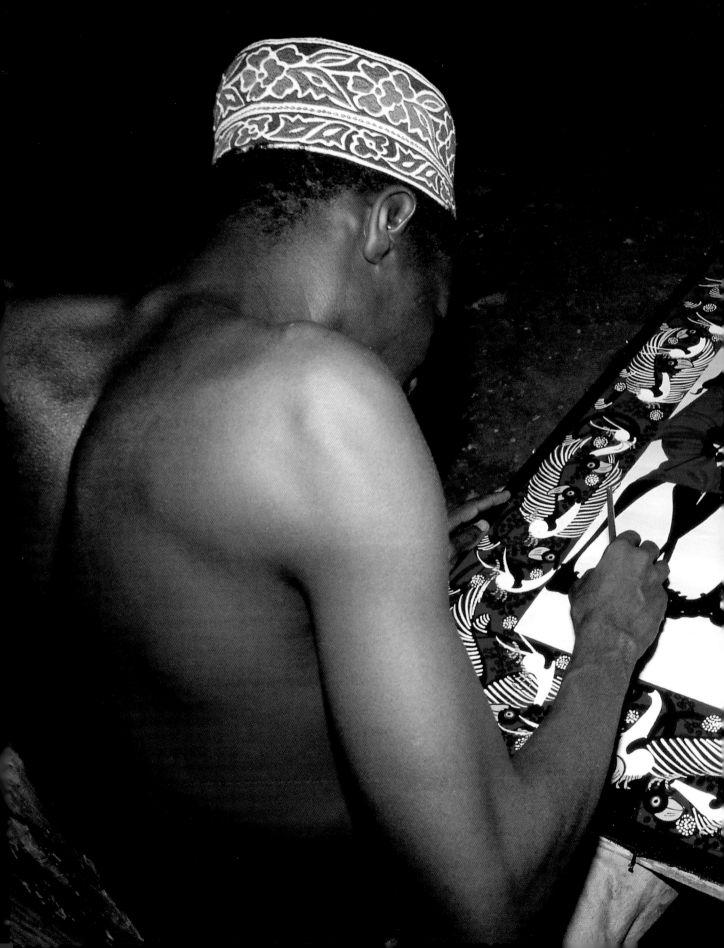

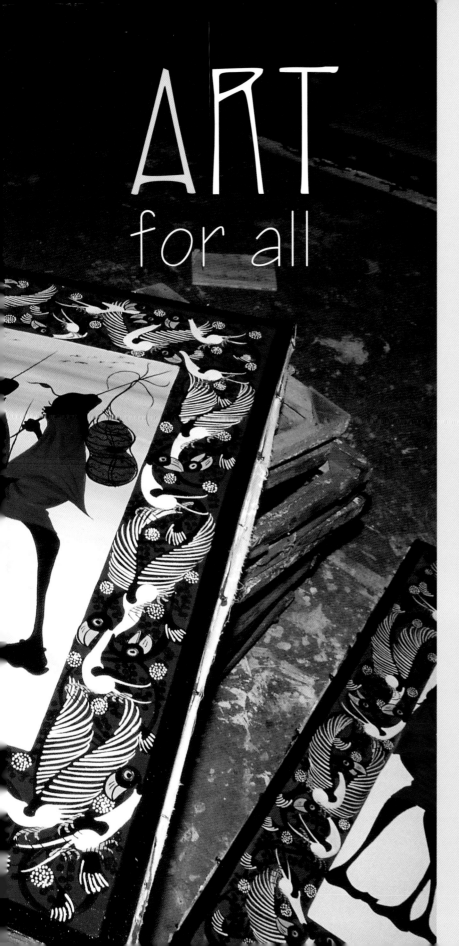

ART
for all

Zanzibar's art scene is an integral part of everyday life and will add colour and warmth to your island experience. It can be seen everywhere: from the more traditional forms, where woodcarvers and weavers labour for both customary and commercial causes in almost every coastal village and rural town, to the many painters and sculptors that work in the backrooms and storefronts of Stone Town. For those in search of the performing artists, the hotels, restaurants and clubs play host to a medley of acts that always bring a sense of reverence and joy to the stage.

LEFT: Tinga tinga art is the most prominent painting style in Zanzibar. Moosa Calima is the artist pictured here.

Tinga tinga art

Anyone spending time in Zanzibar is bound to notice the extremely distinctive artwork that dominates many of the craft and curio stores, adorns the walls and doorways of the busier alleyways in Stone Town and is even sold along the more popular beaches. Always brightly coloured and often painted on lengthy canvasses, this artwork goes by the name of **tinga tinga art**, and it has a fascinating history.

Back in the early 1960s, painting as an art form was almost unheard of in Tanzania. Wood carving, particularly of the well-known Makonde type and a variety of weaving styles and techniques were the popular local artistic pursuits. Because of this, West African artists had moved across the continent to claim the tourism market, successfully selling their works to the burgeoning number of foreigners visiting the country. It was these artists that inspired and influenced a young Tanzanian named **Eduard Said Tingatinga**. Born in the far south of the country in 1937, Tingatinga moved to Dar es Salaam after school and found work with a local medical doctor. He took to painting in his spare time. Using whatever old brushes and paints he could get hold of, he began laying down his artistic impressions of village life on waste cardboard and ceiling boards. In the latter half of the 1960s his art, and that of others, was known as *La Peinture Carré*, or 'square painting'. It was so named because the French-speaking West African artists painted on boxed canvasses that were always 2 foot by 2 foot in size. The local Tanzanian artists followed suit.

But it was a medium of another form that gave his career its commercial boost and introduced his **naïve style** to the Tanzanian art world. He was instructed one day to paint the outside walls of his employer's home. Tingatinga dutifully went about his task, but chose to do so in a manner that was far more expressive than the brief given by his employer. His obvious artistic talents came to light in a bright and expansive masterwork that covered the walls with a collage of animal and human figurines depicting scenes from his village upbringing. Tingatinga was encouraged by the praise for his work, including that from the good doctor himself, and his career as an artist began to flourish. He became the leading pioneer of a unique Tanzanian style of painting and broadened his subject matter beyond village life and animals to include birds and the spiritual world.

It was not until his untimely death in 1972 that his style and techniques would become much copied and formally known as tinga tinga art. He was tragically killed when police in Dar es Salaam mistook the vehicle he was travelling in for a stolen one and opened fire. Fortunately, many of his extended family had learnt from Tingatinga and, after his death, they formed a co-operative and continued painting in his honour. Buoyed by the success of sales, the art form soon flourished on the streets of Dar es Salaam and spread to almost every tourist centre of Tanzania, including Zanzibar. Today's paintings still show the **brimming colours** and unaffected style developed by Tingatinga and their subject matter is still confined to three broad themes: a single animal, village life and the spiritual world (including devils and witchcraft).

Thousands of painters make a living from tinga tinga art. Most outlets that sell these paintings have a studio, either behind the store or nearby, where three or four painters work on a number of pieces simultaneously. Although much of the contemporary tinga tinga art is mass-produced and its subject matter merely copied, there are three world-recognised masters. They have all added elements to its form. George Lilanga, David Mzuguno and Damien Boniface K. Msagula are from mainland Tanzania and have exhibited internationally where their work is widely acclaimed.

For art lovers and collectors, the store to visit in Stone Town is **Real Art** in Gizenga Street. They exhibit the work of the tinga tinga masters, particularly that of George Lilanga, and other well-known local artists. The owners, Pascal Bogaert and Anita Sitta, can provide a wealth of information on the subject.

Other prominent Zanzibari artists are Hashim and Muchi (both recognised masters of woodblock painting) and the world-famous watercolour artist John Da Silva, who lives in Stone Town.

While Zanzibar doesn't have any true art galleries, there is usually a display of up-and-coming local artists in the **Old Dispensary Building** and most of the larger craft and curio stores usually sell paintings as well.

Hassan Kadudu is the most promising of the island's happening artists. Referred to by some as 'Zanzibar's Impressionist', he is fast making a name with his lush and heavy oils that depict life in Stone Town.

Three superb pieces can be seen hanging in the entrance lobby of the Emerson & Green Hotel, while others are displayed in Real Art and his own gallery at the Old Fort. From here, he also runs classes for a growing group of young Zanzibari artists inspired by his works.

Like all true artists, Kadudu can be difficult to track down, but it's worth the hunt as he will personally escort you around Stone Town to view whatever of his works are being displayed in the various stores. Ask for him at the Old Fort, or try him on his e-mail: h_kaduart@hotmail.com

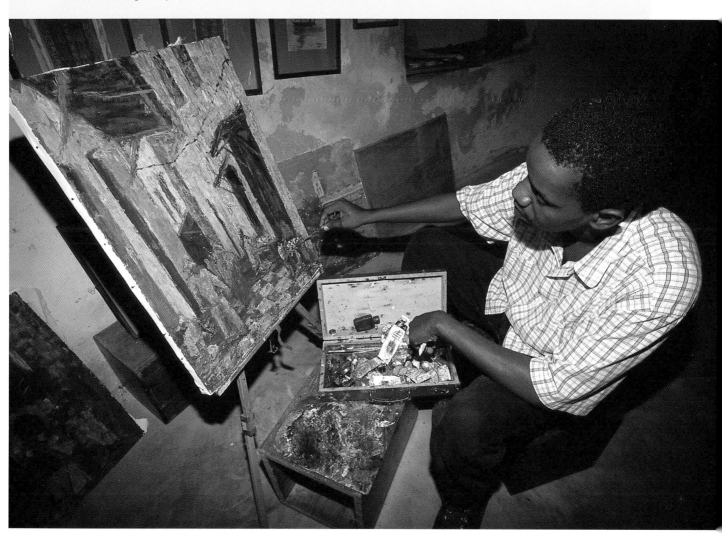

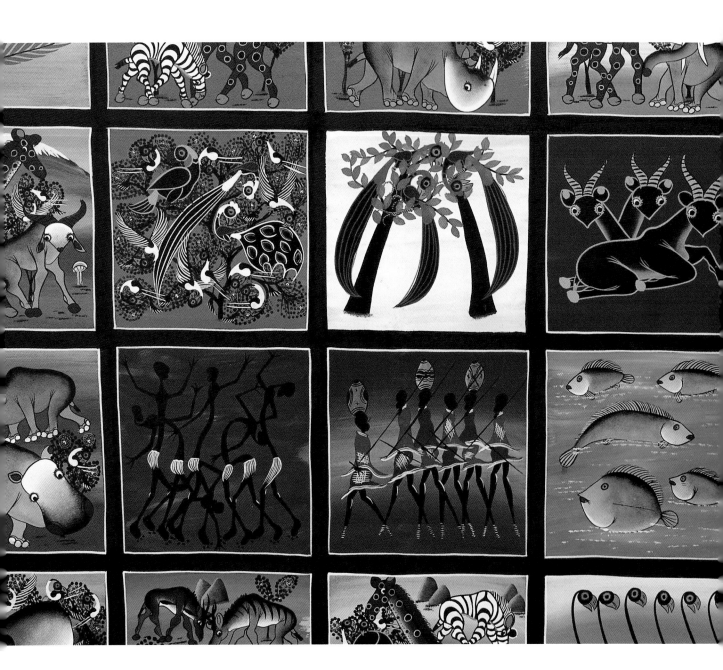

ABOVE: The characteristic naïve style of tinga tinga art mostly depicts village life and the animal and spiritual world.
OPPOSITE: Samora Hassan works with a group of artists who paint a number of canvasses at the same time.

Music

The Zanzibari people are passionate about their music. The best-known genre is *taarab*, which was first introduced by the Arabs as entertainment designed exclusively for the ears of the Sultans. Soon enough it filtered into the populace, with its poetic themes of love and life becoming popular within the local rural communities.

Rooted in Egypt and the Middle East, a traditional *taarab* group may comprise an **orchestra of up to 40 musicians** accompanied by a group of women singers. Traditional instruments include the accordion, a lute or *oud*, a boxed string instrument known as a *ganun* and two small drums known as *tabla*. The more contemporary groups include a double-bass, violins, guitars and sometimes a keyboard. Zanzibar has produced a number of notable *taarab* performers. One of these legends, Bi Kidude, reputedly into her nineties, still occasionally performs in a number of Stone Town clubs and restaurants.

But African music is about **rhythms**, and these have infused their way into *taarab* music over time giving rise to the more localised Swahili version known as *kidumbak*. This Indian and African influenced form is played with fewer instruments, but with more gusto, and is often accompanied by dancers. It is extremely popular at village festivities, local clubs and at parties. During the high season, most of the more popular restaurants host *taarab* and *kidumbak* bands.

The Festival of the Dhow Countries

First held in 1998, this annual festival has now become one of the most popular and influential multicultural art festivals on the African continent. Originally started as a film festival honouring the historic Indian Ocean trading communities and the influence they have had on Zanzibar's culture, it has since grown to **showcase the film, dance, music, poetry and art** from the region, the Middle East and the wider continent.

This is a great time to be in Zanzibar, for the whole island takes on a carnival-like atmosphere with the Old Fort and the waterfront as the hub of the festival. Visitors, performers and exhibitors come from every continent turning Stone Town into a week-long stage with music fiestas, street parades, film premieres, literary forums, exhibitions and workshops. And the vibe is not confined to Stone Town – selected acts from the over 100 films screened and 60 performing arts groups travel into the villages and small towns of the countryside taking the festival to the people.

The festival is usually held at the end of June and into July and, if you're planning to attend, be sure to book your accommodation well in advance as the place gets packed out.

For information on dates and programming, e-mail: ziff@ziff.or.tz or check out their website: www.ziff.or.tz

The Sounds of Wisdom Swahili Music Festival

Held annually in Stone Town during February, this festival brings together some of Zanzibar's most talented **musicians, dancers, acrobats and comedy groups** for four joyous days.

It offers young up-and-coming performers their first stage, showcases new trends in African and, more particularly, Swahili music, and invites established and popular guest stars from the mainland to perform. Everything is on offer – from traditional choirs and *taarab* to the new trends in hip-hop and the emerging Swahili-rap known as 'bongo flava'.

For information on dates and programming, contact Busara Productions: e-mail: busara@zanlink.com

Mwaka Kogwa

This traditional festival has its roots in the ancient Persian religion of Zoroastrianism. It's a four-day-long **Shirazi New Year's celebration**, which, according to the Zoroastrian calendar, occurs during the last weeks of July. While there is much song and dance, a central theme is that of cleansing evil and frustrations from the soul and appeasing God.

Accompanied by singing from the women, men engage in mock fights to symbolise the ridding of tensions within the community so that the new year may begin with harmony and in peace. It takes place in the south of Zanzibar Island, in and around the town of Makunduchi.

Visitors are most welcome, and the best way to view the festival is spend a few days based at Kizimkazi, although those based in Stone Town can do this comfortably as a day trip.

As this is a traditional festival with no official organisation, the best way to confirm dates would be to contact the office of the Dhow Countries Festival at ziff@ziff.or.tz or ZanTours in Stone Town at zantoursinfo@zitec.org

OPPOSITE: Played with rhythm, *kidumbak* is a localised Swahili version of *taarab* music.
ABOVE: Bi Kidude, a legend in the world of *taarab* music, still occasionally performs at venues in Stone Town.

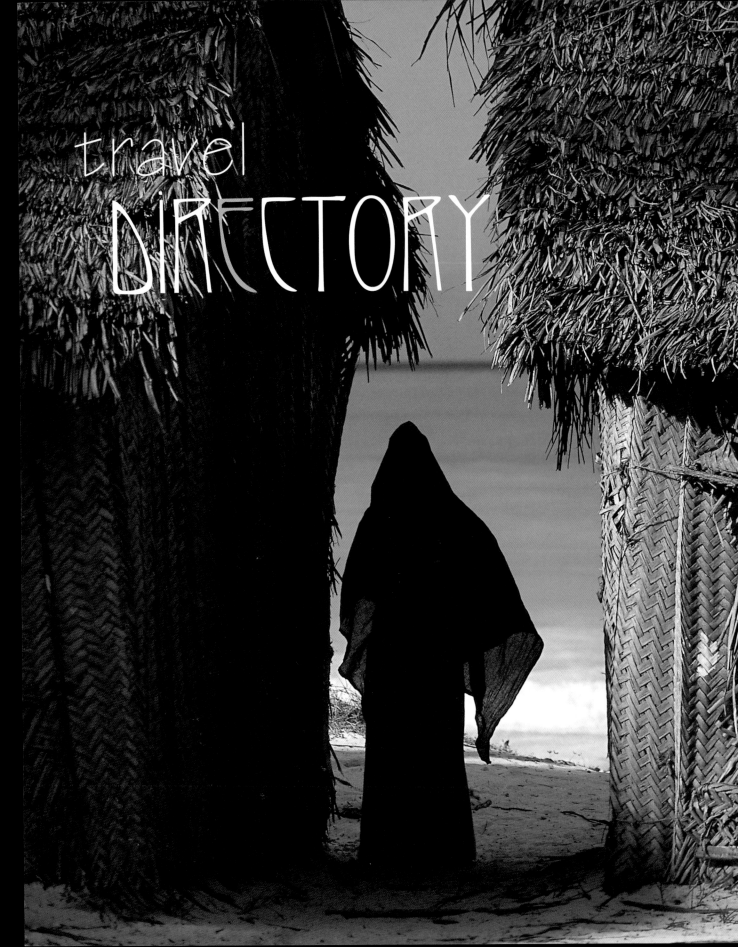

travel
DIRECTORY

LOCAL TIME AND DIALLING CODES

GMT (Greenwich Mean Time) plus 3 hours. International dialling code: +255, then 24 (area code) followed by a 7-digit local number.

WHEN TO TRAVEL

The island has two rainy seasons, the 'short rains' that fall during November and into early December, and the 'long rains' that fall from late March through to early June. The coolest months are June to August (with average low temperatures of between 22°C and 24°C), while the warmest months are November to February (with the average high temperatures between 30°C and 32°C). While Zanzibar has good conditions for travelling during most of the year, the cooler and drier months from July to October are the most comfortable. The months of April and May, when the heavy rains fall, should be avoided, and the hot months from November to January can get uncomfortable, especially if you are staying in accommodation without air conditioning.

VISAS AND ENTRY POINTS

Zanzibar is part of the United Republic of Tanzania with visa applications made through your nearest Tanzania Diplomatic Mission. All visitors require a passport valid for at least six months from date of travel and most countries (except for certain Commonwealth ones) require visas to enter Tanzania. If you are travelling by air, visas can be obtained at international airports on arrival. If you are travelling by road, it is advisable to obtain a visa before arrival. Because of Zanzibar's semi-autonomous standing, visitors will have to show their passports and visas when arriving on the island. The international airport and seaport in Stone Town are the only points of entry. Whenever you leave from here, there will be a charge of some sort – international departure taxes are higher than local ones. These are payable in both foreign and local currency, but cheaper if paid in local shillings.

HEALTH AND MEDICAL

A yellow fever vaccination is required. While this is no longer necessary for entry into Tanzania and Zanzibar, officials of countries to which you next travel will request to see your vaccination certificate upon arrival. The island is classified as a medium to high-risk malaria area. All travellers must consult their local medical practitioner for advice on what malaria prophylactics to take prior to departure. It is worth consulting your doctor about vaccinations for tetanus, hepatitis A and B, typhoid and meningitis. It is not advisable to drink any tap water in Zanzibar or to eat uncooked foods that may have been washed in untreated water. Bottled water is readily available everywhere. It is recommended that travellers take all basic medical requirements and specific medication, as these may not be easily obtainable in Zanzibar.

Contact details for private clinics in Stone Town
ZAMEDIC: +255 24 2233113
Afya Medical Centre:
+255 24 2231228/234927
Zanzibar Medical Group:
+255 24 2231424/233134

EMERGENCY SERVICE NUMBERS

Ambulance: 112
Fire: 111
Police: 999
Medrescue: 999
The national telephone operator: 255

PUBLIC HOLIDAYS

January 1 – New Year's Day
January 12 – Zanzibar Revolution Day
February – Eid-ul-Hajj*
March/April – Good Friday, Easter weekend*
April 26 – Union Day
May 1 – Workers' Day
May – Maulid Day (Prophet Mohammed's Birthday)*
July 7 – Saba Saba Day
August 8th – Farmers' Day
October 14 – Nyerere's Day
October – Eid-ul-Fitr*
December 9 – Independence Day
December 25 – Christmas Day
December 26 – Boxing Day
Dates indicated with * are religious holidays and will change from year to year.

SAFETY AND SECURITY

Zanzibar is generally a relatively safe island to travel with few incidents of serious crime reported. Visitors should be aware, though, that (in Stone Town and along certain beaches) incidents of petty crime do occur where pickpockets and petty thieves operate.

Take the obvious precautions when walking around the capital, and avoid walking alone at night on beaches near towns and villages. If you find yourself at the receiving end of some crime incident, it is advisable to contact the police through your local tour operator, hotel or lodge.

One of the few irritations about Stone Town are the touts, known locally as *papasi* or 'beach boys', who hustle you from many street corners. Strictly speaking, it is illegal to deal with them as they are unregistered operators, but another good reason to avoid them is that some are involved in petty crime and drug dealing.

CURRENCY AND BANKING

The local unit of currency is the Tanzanian Shilling. The following size notes are in circulation: Tsh500, Tsh1 000, Tsh2 000, Tsh5 000 and Tsh10 000. The recommended form of payment for international travellers is by credit card or with cash. Some establishments charge up to 10% on credit card payments.

While traveller's cheques are accepted at the larger hotels and some bureaux, larger commissions are charged on these transactions.

All major cards are accepted at the larger and pricier hotels, lodges and stores. Most smaller shops, particularly those outside of Stone Town, do not have card facilities. US Dollars, British Pounds and Euros are the recommended currencies for those bringing cash. When changing cash, use a *bureau de change* as they offer better rates than banks. Do not change cash with moneychangers on the streets of Stone Town, and don't expect to find any bureaux or banks outside of Stone Town. Non-resident visitors may be asked to show a passport when changing money.

ELECTRICITY

220-240V AC. Most plugs and sockets are of the British three-square-pin format. Adapters are available in some stores in Stone Town. A note of caution – power cuts and surges are common.

INTERNET

Most of the recommended hotels and lodges on Zanzibar Island have internet facilities. There are numerous internet cafes in Stone Town; most of them situated in Kenyatta Road. While they are inexpensive to use, their connections can be unreliable.

TRAVEL TIPS

▶▶ Tourism's low season is generally from April to the end of May, and its high season from July to the end of October. For those travelling on a budget, rates in hotels and lodges and for hired cars and motorbikes can often be negotiated down during the low season. Note that some lodges and hotels close over the low season, so check with your agent.

▶▶ Although the Zanzibar Tourism Authority exists in name, trying to find them or getting information from them are both likely to be fruitless pursuits. Make use of local travel operators or your hotel and lodge staff instead. ZanTours, which is situated in Malindi district in Stone Town, is the largest and most professional operator for local tours and transfers.
Tel: +255 24 2233116/2232692,
e-mail: zantoursinfo@zantours.com

▶▶ Many restaurants may be closed during the day, and others may not serve alcohol, during the period of Ramadan. Shops may also be closed during the afternoon. The dates for the month-long Muslim fast, which are determined by the lunar calendar, differ each year so check with your travel agent or a Tanzanian Embassy.

▶▶ Before booking any accommodation, ask for confirmation about air conditioning and mosquito netting in the rooms. These are must-have items for those not travelling on a tight budget.

▶▶ Local traffic police are always out in force. When making use of a hired car or motorbike, be sure to carry your international driver's license and necessary documentation at all times, as it is highly likely you will be asked for them at police roadblocks.

▶▶ Do not take photographs of sensitive government buildings, residences or airports, and ask permission before taking photographs of the local people.

▶▶ Because of human and industrial pollution, avoid swimming in the sea from the beaches of Stone Town. It is quite safe to swim from the islands offshore of Stone Town.

TOURISM REPRESENTATIVES
ZANAIR: P. O. Box 2113, Zanzibar,
tel: +255 24 2233670/2233768,
e-mail: zanair@zitec.org,
website: www.zanair.com

Zanzibar Association of Tourism Investors (ZATI):
P. O. Box 2578, Zanzibar,
tel: +255 747 475065,
e-mail: info@zati.org,
website: www.zati.org

Zanzibar Commission for Tourism: P. O. Box 1410, Zanzibar or Amaan Road, Zanzibar Town,
tel: +255 24 2233485,
e-mail: zanzibartourism@zanzibartourism.net,
website: www.zanzibartourism.net

The following websites provide valuable information:
www.zanzibar-web.com,
www.zanzibar.net
www.zanzibartourism.net

TOUR OPERATORS
African Encounters: 23A, 1st Ave East, Parktown North, Johannesburg, South Africa,
tel: +27 11 8803079,
e-mail: info@africanencounters.com,
website: www.encounterzanzibar.com

Invent Africa: Whalley House, Marsh Memorial Homes, Rondebosch, Cape Town,
South Africa, tel: +27 21 6856219,
e-mail: info@inventafrica.com,
website: www.inventafrica.com

ZanTours: P. O. Box 2560, Zanzibar,
Tanzania, tel/fax: +255 24 2233116/ 2233042/2232692,
e-mail: zantoursinfo@zitec.org/ zantoursinfo@zantours.com,
website: www.zantours.com

HOTELS AND LODGES
Stone Town
Chavda Hotel: P. O. Box 540, Zanzibar,
tel: +255 24 2232115,
e-mail: chavda@zanzinet.com

Coco de Mer Hotel: P. O. Box 2363,
Shangani, Stone Town,
tel: +255 24 2230852,
e-mail: cocodemer_znz@yahoo.com

Dhow Palace Hotel: P. O. Box 3974, Zanzibar,
tel: +255 24 2233012/2230304,
e-mail: dhowpalace@zanjcom.com

Emerson & Green: P. O. Box 3417, Zanzibar,
tel: +255 747 423266,
e-mail: emerson&green@zitec.org,
website: www.emerson-green.com

Karibu Inn: P. O. Box 3228, Forodhani St, Stone Town, tel: +255 24 2233058,
e-mail: karibuinn@zanzinet.com

Mtoni Marine Centre: P. O. Box 992, Zanzibar,
tel: +255 24 2250140,
e-mail: zanzibar@coastal.cc

Tembo House Hotel: P. O. Box 3974, Zanzibar,
tel: +255 24 2233005/2232069,
e-mail: tembo@zitec.org,
website: www.tembohotel.com

The Africa House Hotel: P. O. Box 3246, Shangani, tel: +255 747 432340, e-mail: theafricahouse@yahoo.com

Zanzibar Beach Resort: P. O. Box 2586, Mazizini, tel: +255 24 2236033/2236044, e-mail: bookings@zanzibarbeachresort.net, website: www.zanzibarbeachresort.net

Zanzibar Serena Inn: P. O. Box 4151, Stone Town, tel: +255 24 2233587, e-mail: gmahimbo@serena.co.tz, website: www.serenahotels.com

The north
Baobab Beach Bungalows:
P. O. Box 2632,
Nungwi, Zanzibar,
tel: +255 747 416964 or 24 2236315,
e-mail: baobabnungwi@zanzinet.com,
website: www.baobabbeachbungalows.com

La Gemma dell' Est: P. O. Box 4700, Zanzibar, tel: +255 24 2239452, e-mail: renco-zan@renco.it

Ras Nungwi Beach Hotel: P. O. Box 1784, Zanzibar, tel: +255 24 2233767/2232512, e-mail: rasnungwi@zanzibar.net, website: www.rasnungwi.com

The east
Bluebay Beach Resort: P. O. Box 3276, Zanzibar, tel: +255 24 2240240/1/2, e-mail: reservations@bluebayzanzibar.com, website: www.bluebayzanzibar.com

Bravo Club: P. O. Box 4095, Zanzibar, tel: +255 747 414480/1, e-mail: sckiwengwa@renthotel.org

Coral Reef Resort: P. O. Box 65, Mahonda, Zanzibar, tel: +255 747 415549/414040, e-mail: coralreef@zanzinet.com, website: www.zanzibar-coralreef.com

Mapenzi Beach Club: P. O. Box 100, Mahonda, Zanzibar, tel: +255 741 325985, e-mail: genman@planhotelzanzibar.com

Matemwe Bungalows: P. O. Box 3275, Zanzibar, tel: +255 747 425788, e-mail: info@matemwe.com, website: www.matemwe.com

Sea Club Kiwengwa: P. O. Box 4095, Zanzibar, tel: +255 747 414447, e-mail: bckiwengwa@renthotel.org

Shooting Star Lodge: P. O. Box 3076, Zanzibar, tel: +255 747 414166, UK Reservations: +44 1242 222027, e-mail: star@zanzibar.org, website: www.zanzibar.org/star

Venta Club: P. O. Box 13, Zanzibar, tel: +255 747 414845, e-mail: ricevemento@hotmail.com

Vera Club: P. O. Box 2529, Kiwengwa, Zanzibar, tel: +255 747 414988, e-mail: veraclubznz@zitec.org

The southeast
Breezes Beach Club: P. O. Box 1361, Zanzibar, tel: +255 747 415049, e-mail: info@breezes-zanzibar.com, website: www.breezes-zanzibar.com

Dongwe Club: P. O. Box 1283, Zanzibar, tel: +255 24 2240250/1/2, e-mail: manager@dongweclub.co.tz, website: www.dongweclub.co.tz

Karafuu Hotel Beach Resort: P. O. Box 71, Zanzibar, tel: +255 747 413647, e-mail: karafuuhotel@zanzinet.com, website: www.karafuuhotel.com

Pongwe Beach Hotel: P. O. Box 297, Zanzibar, tel: +255 747 413973,

ail: info@pongwe.com,
bsite: www.pongwe.com

Palms: P. O. Box 1298, Zanzibar,
tel: +255 747 437007 or 748 203092,
e-mail: info@palms-zanzibar.com,
website: www.palms-zanzibar.com

Sultan Palace: P. O. Box 4074, Zanzibar,
tel: +255 24 2240173/2240264,
e-mail: sultanpalace@swiftkenya.com

Stone Town islands
Chapwani Island: P. O. Box 3248, Zanzibar,
tel: +255 744 858111,
e-mail: chapwani@zitec.org,
website: www.chapwaniisland.com

Chumbe Island Coral Park: P. O. Box 3203,
Zanzibar, tel: +255 54 231040
or 747 413582,
e-mail: chumbe@twiga.com,
website: www.chumbeisland.com

Pemba Island
Fundu Lagoon: P. O. Box 3945, Zanzibar,
tel +255 24 2232926,
e-mail: fundu@africaonline.co.tz,
website: www.fundulagoon.com

Mnemba Island
Mnemba Island Lodge: Private Bag X27,
Benmore, 2010, Johannesburg, South Africa,
tel: +27 11 8094300,
e-mail: information@ccafrica.com or
ccafricazanzibar@zanzinet,
website: www.ccafrica.com

DIVING OPERATORS
Bahari Divers: P. O. Box 204, Zanzibar,
tel: +255 748 254786,
e-mail: baharidivers@hotmail.com,
website: www.zanzibar-diving.com

Mnemba Dive School: For contact details see
Mnemba Island Lodge, or contact them in
Zanzibar at tel: +255 747 438656 or
741 335853,

One Ocean: P. O. Box 608, Zanzibar,
tel: +255 24 2238374 or 742 750161,
e-mail: oneocean@zanlink.com,
website: www.zanzibaroneocean.com

Ras Nungwi Beach Hotel: P. O. Box1784, Zanzibar,
tel: +255 24 2233767/2232512,
e-mail: rasnungwi@zanzibar.net,
website: www.rasnungwi.com

AIR CHARTER
Tropical Air: P. O. Box 3188, Zanzibar,
tel: +255 24 2232511/2234819,
e-mail: tropic@zanzinet.com

CAR RENTAL
Forodhani Car Hire: P. O. Box 4041, Zanzibar,
tel: +255 747 410186/413287,
e-mail: allypillow@hotmail.com

INVESTMENT OPPORTUNITIES
Zanzibar Investments: Promotion Agency (ZIPA):
P. O. Box 2286, Zanzibar,
Tel: +255 24 2233026/2233758,
e-mail: zipaznz@zanzinet.com,
website: www.investzanzibar.com

Suggested reading

2001 Census of Industrial Production, 2001 (Office of Chief Government Statistician, Zanzi[

African Studies – The Shell Money Of The Slave Trade, 2003, Jan Hogendorn; Marion Jc
    (Cambridge University)

Dhows and The Colonial Economy of Zanzibar, 1860–1970, 2004, Erik Gilbert (Ohio U

Dive Sites of Kenya and Tanzania, 1997, A. Koornhof (New Holland)

East Africa In The 50's, 1998, Agency Environment; S. J. Colman; Sidney Coleman
    (I. B. Tauris & Company)

Eastern African Studies – Pastimes and Politics – Culture, Community, And Identity in Post-
    Abolition Urban Zanzibar, 1890–1945, 2002, Laura Fair (Ohio University)

Eastern African Studies – The History & Conservation of Zanzibar Stone Town, 1995,
    Prof. Abdul Sheriff (Ohio University)

Eastern African Studies – Zanzibar under Colonial Rule, 1991, Prof. Abdul Sheriff (Ohio University)

Globetrotter Travel Guide – Tanzania, 2003, Graham Mercer (New Holland)

Globetrotter Travel Map – Tanzania, 2003, Graham Mercer (New Holland)

Historical Dictionary Of Tanzania, 1997, Rodger Yeager; Thomas P. Ofcansky (Scarecrow)

Lake Regions Of Central Africa, The (Volume II) – From Zanzibar to Lake Tanganyika, 2001,
    Richard Francis Burton (Stackpole Books)

Livingstone's Tribe – A Journey from Zanzibar to the Cape, 2000, Stephen Taylor (Flamingo)

Lonely Planet – Tanzania, 2002, Mary Fitzpatrick (Lonely Planet)

Meeting the Invisible Man – Travels and Magic in West Africa, 2002, Toby Green (Phoenix)

Revolution in Zanzibar – An American's Cold War Tale, 2002, Donald Petterson (Westview)

Southern/East Africa – Road Atlas, 2002 (Map Studio)

Sowing the Wind – Zanzibar and Pemba before the Revolution, 2001, Maulid M. Haj (Gallery)

Tanzania 2002 Population and Housing Census – General Report, 2002 (National Bureau of
    Statistics, Tanzania)

Tippoo Tib – The Story of His Career in Zanzibar and Central Africa, 1969, Dr. Heinrich Brode
    (Afro-Am)

Wonder Safaris, The, 2003, Adam Levin (Struik)

Zanzibar and Stone Town – An Architectural Exploration, 2001, Prof. Abdul Sheriff; Javed Jafferji
    (Gallery)

Zanzibar – An Essential Guide, 1999, Mame McCutchin (Gallery)

Zanzibar – City, Island And Coast (Volume Two), 2003, Richard Francis Burton
    (University Press of the Pacific)

Zanzibar in Contemporary Times, 1969, Robert N Lyne (Negro Universities)

Zanzibar Style, 2001, Javed Jafferji (Gallery)

Glossary

The   *ra* – The Arabic name for Pemba.

board game played with seed or bean playing pieces.

A street-level outside bench built along the front walls of a house.

A long black overdress worn by devout Muslim women.

dala dala – A light truck that has been converted for use as a taxi.

dhow – A general term used to describe all wooden boats driven by sails.

hijab – Black headgear, worn by devout Muslim women, that leaves only the eyes exposed.

jahazi – The largest of the dhows used for carrying heavy cargo.

kanzu – A long flowing white tunic worn by Muslim men.

karibu – The Kiswahili word for welcome.

kaskazi – The hot season between December and March.

khanga – Bright rectangular cotton cloth worn mostly by women as wrap-around clothing.

kidumbak – A more localised Swahili version of taarab music.

kipupwe – The cool mid-year season.

kofia – A small flat-topped hat worn by Muslim men.

masika – The heavy rain season between March and May.

mchawis – In local custom, the name given to those that practise as wizards and witches.

mgangas – A traditional healer and someone who is the purveyor of good spiritual deeds.

mzungu – A person of European descent, or, more informally, a white person.

ngalawa – The smaller twin-hulled dhows used as fishing craft.

sawahil – An Arabic word meaning 'of the coast'.

Shetani – In local custom, the spirit that is associated with all things evil and sinister.

shisha pipe – A traditional bowl-shaped pipe that originates from the Middle East.

taarab – Traditional Arab music that has its roots in Egypt and the Middle East.

tinga tinga art – The distinctive naïve art style seen throughout the archipelago depicting mostly village life, and the animal and spiritual world. The name is taken from Eduard Said Tingatinga.

Unguja – The local name for Zanzibar Island.

vuli – The short rains in November.

Zain Za'l Bar – Arabic phrase meaning 'fair is the land/coast'.

Zinj el-Barr – Arabic phrase meaning 'land/coast of the blacks'.

Zanzibar speaks of the romance of lazy languid days spent sun-soaking on palm-lined beaches and sipping cocktails at sunset.

Author's info

IAN MICHLER, a stockbroker by profession, left the world of finance in 1989 to live and work in the Okavango Delta. He has 15 years of guiding experience, mostly in Botswana, Namibia and Zimbabwe but also in parts of East Africa – conducting big game, birding, adventure and photographic safaris. When not on safari, he works as a photojournalist, writing on conservation, wildlife and travel issues, predominantly for the magazines *Africa Geographic* and *Africa Birds and Birding*. He has worked as a researcher and field co-ordinator on numerous natural history television documentaries. His work also takes him to Zambia, Malawi, Mozambique and Uganda, where he has travelled extensively. Ian has three previous books to his credit, *This is Mozambique*, *Mozambique – A Visual Souvenir* and *BOTWSWANA The Insider's Guide*. He is a past category winner in the Agfa Wildlife Photographic Awards.

To travel with Ian as your guide or receive advice on travelling in southern and East Africa, you can contact him at: Invent Africa, tel: +27 21 6856219, email: info@inventafrica.com, website: www.inventafrica.com

Other books by Ian Michler

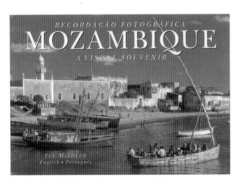

Mozambique – A Visual Souvenir

The blue water of the Indian Ocean, a warm tropical sun and endless beaches framed with tropical vegetation are but some of the attractions of Mozambique. In *Mozambique – A Visual Souvenir*, the country's highlights are shown, such as its diverse cultures and its offshore islands, with beautiful full-colour photographs.

Botswana – The Insider's Guide

Botswana boasts some of southern Africa's most glorious and unspoiled safari destinations, with a staggering array of wildlife and pristine habitats. Most spectacular of the country's natural treasures is the Okavango Delta, home to unsurpassed animal and bird life, which you can discover on foot, in a 4x4 vehicle or on a leisurely *mokoro* trip. But wildlife is not all Botswana has to offer. *The Insider's Guide* takes you on a journey through a country that

has one of the most vibrant economies in the region and is home to a thriving arts and cultural scene. It also gives you invaluable insight into the life and people: practical details on the best overland trips you can take, the ideal camps and lodges for a safari, and wonderful insider tips on where to find the best arts, crafts, festivals and music on your travels.

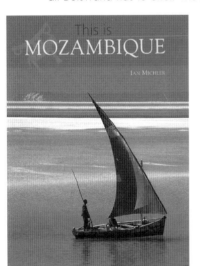

This is Mozambique

In *This is Mozambique*, the country's history, its people, economy, cultures, main cities and major tourist drawcards (including game reserves such as the splendid Gorongosa Park), its sea life and the beautiful Bazaruto, Inhaca and Benguerra islands are discussed in detail in a comprehensive introduction.

The second half of the book is divided into the southern, central and northern regions of Mozambique and takes readers on a full-colour photographic journey through the country, as well as showcasing the activities in which visitors can participate, such as diving and snorkelling, deep-sea fishing, and a host of other watersports.